READY NOTES

for use with

FOUNDATIONS OF
FINANCIAL
MANAGEMENT

Eighth Edition

Stanley B. Block
Texas Christian University
Geoffrey A. Hirt
DePaul University

D1530919

IRWIN
Chicago • Bogotá • Boston • Buenos Aires • Caracas
London • Madrid • Mexico City • Sydney • Toronto

Printed in the United States of America.

ISBN 0–256–14621–7

1 2 3 4 5 6 7 8 9 0 EB 3 2 1 0 9 8 7 6

TABLE OF CONTENTS

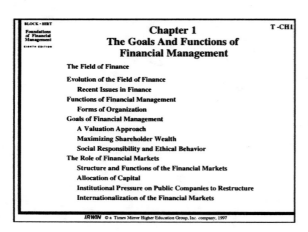

BLOCK · HIRT
Foundations of Financial Management
EIGHTH EDITION

Chapter 1
The Goals And Functions of
Financial Management

T -CH1

IRWIN © a Times Mirror Higher Education Group, Inc. company, 1997

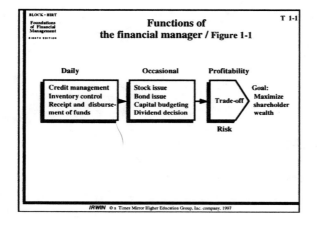

BLOCK · HIRT
Foundations of Financial Management
EIGHTH EDITION

Functions of
the financial manager / Figure 1-1

T 1-1

Daily | Occasional | Profitability

Credit management
Inventory control
Receipt and disbursement of funds

Stock issue
Bond issue
Capital budgeting
Dividend decision

Trade-off

Risk

Goal:
Maximize
shareholder
wealth

IRWIN © a Times Mirror Higher Education Group, Inc. company, 1997

BLOCK • HIRT

Foundations
of Financial
Management

EIGHTH EDITION

T -CH2

Chapter 2
Review of Accounting

BLOCK • HIRT

Foundations
of Financial
Management

EIGHTH EDITION

T 2-1

Part II Financial analysis
and planning

KRAMER CORPORATION
Income Statement
For the Year Ended Statement December 31, 1997

1.	Sales	$ 2,000,000
2.	Cost of goods sold	1,500,000
3.	Gross Profits	500,000
4.	Selling and administrative expense	270,000
5.	Depreciation expense	50,000
6.	Operating profit (EBIT)*. . . .	180,000
7.	Interest expense	20,000
8.	Earnings before taxes (EBT) . . .	160,000
9.	Taxes	49,500
10.	Earnings after taxes (EAT) . . .	110,500
11.	Preferred stock dividends	10,500
12.	Earnings available to common stockholders	100,000
		100,000
13.	Shares outstanding	100,000
14.	Earnings per share	$1.00

*Earnings before interest and taxes.

BLOCK • HIRT

Foundations
of Financial
Management

EIGHTH EDITION

T 2-2

Part II Financial Analysis
and Planning

Price-earnings ratios for selected U.S. companies / Table 2-3

Corporation	Industry	Jan. 2 1983	Jan. 2 1986	Jan. 2 1990	Jan. 2 1993	Jan. 2 1996
Apple	Computers	30	12	11	13	9
Coca-Cola	Beverages	13	17	20	25	34
Disney	Entertainment	25	20	19	26	23
Liz Claiborne . . .	Clothing	13	19	11	19	17
McDonald's	Restaurants	10	16	18	20	24
Nations Bank . . .	Banking	7	10	9	10	10
Phelps Dodge . . .	Copper	6	8	4	17	7
Southwest Air . . .	Airlines	20	14	15	38	21
Texas Utilities . . .	Public utilities	6	7	8	15	14
Wal-Mart	Retail	26	28	24	39	18
Standard & Poor's						
(500 Stock Index) . .		11	14	15	22	17

2

Review of accounting / Table 2-4
(first part)

KRAMER CORPORATION
Statement of Financial Position (Balance Sheet)
December 31, 1997

Assets

Current assets:

Cash			40,000
Marketable securities			10,000
Accounts receivable	$	220,000	
Less: Allowance for bad debts . .		20,000	200,000
Inventory			180,000
Prepaid expenses			20,000
Total current assets			450,000

Other assets:

Investments			50,000

Fixed assets:

Plant and equipment, original cost. . .		1,100,000	
Less: Accumulated depreciation . .		600,000	
Net plant and equipment			500,000
Total assets			$1,000,000

Review of accounting / Table 2-4
(final part)

Liabilities and Stockholders' Equity

Current liabilities:

Accounts payable	$ 80,000
Notes payable	100,000
Accrued expenses	30,000
Total current liabilities.	210,000

Long-term liabilities:

Bonds payable, 2010	90,000
Total liabilities	300,000

Stockholders' equity:

Preferred stock, $100 par value, 500 shares. . .	50,000
Common stock, $1 par value, 100,000 shares . .	100,000
Captial paid in excess of par (common stock) . .	250,000
Retained earnings	300,000
Total stockholders' equity	700,000
Total liabilities and stockholders' equity	$ 1,000,000

Review of Accounting

Comparison of market value to book value per share in October 1995 / Table 2-5

Corporation	Market Value per Share	Book Value per Share	Ratio of Market Value to Book Value
Microsoft	$92.50	9.10	10.16
Pfizer	53.00	7.55	7.02
Biogen	61.00	10.30	5.92
Home Depot	43.25	10.50	4.12
Monsanto	99.75	29.45	3.39
Sizzler Int.	5.75	6.35	.91
R. J. Nabisco	29.25	34.00	.86
Farah, Inc.	6.75	9.05	.75
Niagara Mohawk . . .	12.00	17.40	.69
Edison Brothers . . .	5.50	16.35	.34

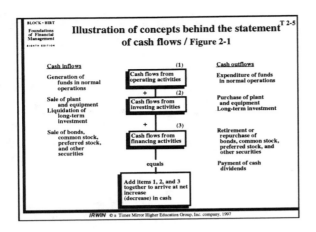

Illustration of concepts behind the statement of cash flows / Figure 2-1

T 2-5

BLOCK · HIRT
Foundations of Financial Management
EIGHTH EDITION

Cash inflows		Cash outflows
Generation of funds in normal operations	(1) Cash flows from operating activities	Expenditure of funds in normal operations
Sale of plant and equipment Liquidation of long-term investment	+ (2) Cash flows from investing activities	Purchase of plant and equipment Long-term investment
Sale of bonds, common stock, preferred stock, and other securities	+ (3) Cash flows from financing activities	Retirement or repurchase of bonds, common stock, preferred stock, and other securities
	equals	Payment of cash dividends
	Add items 1, 2, and 3 together to arrive at net increase (decrease) in cash	

IRWIN © a Times Mirror Higher Education Group, Inc. company, 1997

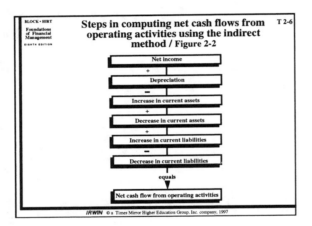

Steps in computing net cash flows from operating activities using the indirect method / Figure 2-2

T 2-6

BLOCK · HIRT
Foundations of Financial Management
EIGHTH EDITION

Net income
+
Depreciation
−
Increase in current assets
+
Decrease in current assets
+
Increase in current liabilities
−
Decrease in current liabilities
equals
Net cash flow from operating activities

IRWIN © a Times Mirror Higher Education Group, Inc. company, 1997

BLOCK · HIRT
Foundations of Financial Management
EIGHTH EDITION

T 2-7

Table 2-6 (first part)

KRAMER CORPORATION
Comparative Balance Sheets

Assets		Year-End 1996	Year-End 1997
Current assets:			
Cash	$	30,000	$ 40,000
Marketable securities		10,000	10,000
Accounts receivable (net)		170,000	200,000
Inventory		160,000	180,000
Prepaid expenses		30,000	20,000
Total current assets		400,000	450,000
Investments (long term)		20,000	50,000
Plant and equipment		1,000,000	1,100,000
Less: Accumulated depreciation		550,000	600,000
Net plant and equipment		450,000	500,000
Total assets	$	870,000	$ 1,000,000

IRWIN © a Times Mirror Higher Education Group, Inc. company, 1997

BLOCK · HIRT

Foundations
of Financial
Management
EIGHTH EDITION

T 2-7

Table 2-6 (final part)

KRAMER CORPORATION
Comparative Balance Sheets

Liabilities and Stockholders' Equity	Year-End 1996	Year-End 1997
Current liabilities:		
Accounts payable	$ 45,000	$ 80,000
Notes payable	100,000	100,000
Accrued expenses	35,000	30,000
Total current liabilities	180,000	210,000
Long-term liabilities:		
Bonds payable, 1998	40,000	90,000
Total liabilities	220,000	300,000
Stockholders' equity:		
Preferred stock, $100 par value	50,000	50,000
Common stock, $1 par value	100,000	100,000
Captial paid in excess of par	250,000	250,000
Retained earnings	250,000	300,000
Total stockholders' equity	650,000	700,000
Total liabilities and stockholders' equity	$ 870,000	$ 1,000,000

BLOCK · HIRT

Foundations
of Financial
Management
EIGHTH EDITION

T 2-8

Cash flows from operating activities / Table 2-7

Net income (earnings after taxes) (Table 2-1)		$110,500
Adjustments to determine cash flow from operating activities:		
Add back depreciation (Table 2-1)	50,000	
Increase in accounts receivable (Table 2-6)	(30,000)	
Increase in inventory (Table 2-6)	(20,000)	
Decrease in prepaid expenses (Table 2-6)	10,000	
Increase in accounts payable (Table 2-6)	35,000	
Decrease in accrued expenses (Table 2-6)	(5,000)	
Total adjustments		40,000
Net cash flows from operating activities		$150,500

BLOCK · HIRT

Foundations
of Financial
Management
EIGHTH EDITION

T 2-9

Table 2-10 (first part)

KRAMER CORPORATION
Statement of Cash Flows
For the Year Ending December 31, 1997

Cash flows from operating activities:		
Net income (earnings after taxes)		$ 110,500
Adjustments to determine cash flow from operating activities:		
Add back depreciation	50,000	
Increase in accounts receivable	(30,000)	
Increase in inventory	(20,000)	
Decrease in prepaid expenses	10,000	
Increase in accounts payable	35,000	
Decrease in accrued expenses	(5,000)	
Total adjustments		40,000
Net cash flows from operating activities		$ 150,500

BLOCK · HIRT
Foundations
of Financial
Management
EIGHTH EDITION

Table 2-10 (final part)

Cash flows from investing activities:		
Increase in investments (long-term securities) . . .	(30,000)	
Increase in plant and equipment	(100,000)	
Net cash flows from investing activities		($130,000)
Cash flows from financing activities:		
Increase in bonds payable	50,000	
Preferred stock dividends paid	(10,500)	
Common stock dividends paid	(50,000)	
Net cash flows from financing activities . . .		($10,500)
Net increase (decrease) in cash flows		$10,000

BLOCK · HIRT
Foundations
of Financial
Management
EIGHTH EDITION

Comparison of accounting and cash flows /
Table 2-11 (first part)

	Year 1	
	(A) Accounting Flows	(B) Cash Flows
Earnings before depreciation and taxes (EBDT) . .	$1,000	$1,000
Depreciation	100	100
Earnings before taxes (EBT)	900	900
Taxes	300	300
Earnings after taxes (EAT)	$600	600
Purchase of equipment		-500
Depreciation charged without cash outlay . . .		+100
Cash flow		$ 200

BLOCK · HIRT
Foundations
of Financial
Management
EIGHTH EDITION

Comparison of accounting and cash flows /
Table 2-11 (final part)

	Year 2	
	(A) Accounting Flows	(B) Cash Flows
Earnings before depreciation and taxes (EBDT) . .	$1,000	$1,000
Depreciation	100	100
Earnings before taxes (EBT)	900	900
Taxes	300	300
Earnings after taxes (EAT)	$ 600	600
Depreciation charged without cash outlay . . .		+100
Cash flow		$ 700

Chapter 3
Financial Analysis

Ratio Analysis
    Classification System
    The Analysis
    Trend Analysis
Impact of Inflation on Financial Analysis
    An Illustration
    Disinflation Effect
Other Elements of Distortion in Reported Income
    Explanation of Discrepancies
    Net Income
    America Online Example

Classification System

We will separate 13 significant ratios into four primary categories.

A. Profitability Ratios.
    1. Profit margin.
    2. Return on assets (investment).
    3. Return on equity.
B. Asset utilization ratios.
    4. Receivable turnover.
    5. Average collection period.
    6. Inventory turnover.
    7. Fixed asset turnover.
    8. Total asset turnover.
C. Liquidity ratios.
    9. Current ratio.
    10. Quick ratio.
D. Debt utilization ratios.
    11. Debt to total assets.
    12. Times interest earned.
    13. Fixed charge coverage.

Financial Statement
for ratio analysis / Table 3-1 (first part)

SAXTON COMPANY

Income Statement
For the Year Ended December 31, 1997

Sales (all on credit)	$ 4,000,000
Cost of goods sold	3,000,000
Gross Profit	1,000,000
Selling and administrative expense*	450,000
Operating profit	550,000
Interest expense	50,000
Extraordinary loss	200,000
Net income before taxes	300,000
Taxes (33%)	100,000
Net income	$ 200,000

* Includes $50,000 in lease payments.

BLOCK · HIRT
Foundations
of Financial
Management
EIGHTH EDITION

Financial Statement for
ratio analysis / Table 3-1 (final part)

Balance Sheet
As of December 31, 1997
Assets

Cash	$ 30,000
Marketable securities	50,000
Accounts receivable	350,000
Inventory	370,000
Total current assets	800,000
Net plant and equipment	800,000
Total assets	$1,600,000

Liabilities and Stockholders' Equity

Accounts payable	$ 50,000
Notes payable	250,000
Total current liabilities	300,000
Long-term liabilities	300,000
Total liabilities	600,000
Common stock	400,000
Retained earnings	600,000
Total liabilities and stockholders' equity	$1,600,000

BLOCK · HIRT
Foundations
of Financial
Management
EIGHTH EDITION

Profitability ratios

	Saxton Company	Industry Average
1. Profit margin = $\dfrac{\text{Net income}}{\text{sales}}$	$\dfrac{\$200,000}{\$4,000,000} = 5\%$	6.7%

2. Return on assets (investment) =

a. $\dfrac{\text{Net income}}{\text{Total assets}}$ $\dfrac{\$200,000}{\$1,600,000} = 12.5\%$ 10%

b. $\dfrac{\text{Net income}}{\text{Sales}} \times \dfrac{\text{Sales}}{\text{Total assets}}$ $5\% \times 2.5 = 12.5\%$ $6.7\% \times 1.5 = 10\%$

3. Return on equity =

a. $\dfrac{\text{Net income}}{\text{Stockholders' equity}}$ $\dfrac{\$200,000}{\$1,000,000} = 20\%$ 15%

b. $\dfrac{\text{Return on assets (investment)}}{(1 - \text{Debt/Assets})}$ $\dfrac{0.125}{1 - 0.375} = 20\%$ $\dfrac{0.10}{1 - 0.33} = 15\%$

BLOCK · HIRT
Foundations
of Financial
Management
EIGHTH EDITION

DuPont analysis /Figure 3-1

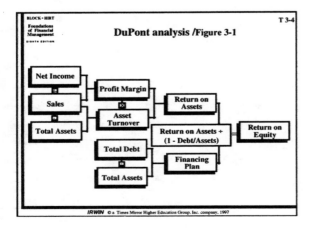

Position of
Wal-Mart vs. Dillard's using the
DuPont method of analysis, 1995 / Table 3-2

Company	Profit Margin ×	Asset Turnover =	Return on Assets +	(1 – Debt/Assets) =	Return on Equity
Wal-Mart	3.1% ×	2.6 =	8.1% +	(1 – 0.503) =	16.3%
Dillard's	4.4% ×	1.3 =	5.7% +	(1 – 0.436) =	10.1%

Asset utilization ratios (first part)

	Saxton Company	Industry Average
4. Receivables turnover = $\dfrac{\text{Sales (credit)}}{\text{Receivables}}$	$\dfrac{\$4,000,000}{\$350,000}$ = 11.4	10 times
5. Average collection period = $\dfrac{\text{Accounts receivable}}{\text{Average daily credit sales}}$	$\dfrac{\$350,000}{\$11,111}$ = 32	36 days
6. Inventory turnover = $\dfrac{\text{Sales}}{\text{Inventory}}$	$\dfrac{\$4,000,000}{\$370,000}$ = 10.8	7 times

---

Asset utilization ratios (final part)

	Saxton Company	Industry Average
7. Fixed asset turnover = $\dfrac{\text{Sales}}{\text{Fixed assets}}$	$\dfrac{\$4,000,000}{\$800,000}$ = 5	5.4 times
8. Total asset turnover = $\dfrac{\text{Sales}}{\text{Total assets}}$	$\dfrac{\$4,000,000}{\$1,600,000}$ = 2.5	1.5 times

BLOCK • HIRT
Foundations
of Financial
Management
EIGHTH EDITION
T 3-7

Liquidity ratios

	Saxton Company	Industry Average
9. Current ratio =		
$\dfrac{\text{Current assets}}{\text{Current liabilities}}$	$\dfrac{\$800,000}{\$300,000} = 2.67$	2.1
10. Quick ratio =		
$\dfrac{\text{Current assets – Inventory}}{\text{Current liabilities}}$	$\dfrac{\$430,000}{\$300,000} = 1.43$	1.0

IRWIN © a Times Mirror Higher Education Group, Inc. company. 1997

BLOCK • HIRT
Foundations
of Financial
Management
EIGHTH EDITION
T 3-8

Debt utilization ratios

	Saxton Company	Industry Average
11. Debt to total asets =		
$\dfrac{\text{Total debt}}{\text{Total assets}}$	$\dfrac{\$600,000}{\$1,600,000} = 37.5\%$	33%
12. Times interest earned =		
$\dfrac{\text{Income before interest and taxes}}{\text{Interest}}$	$\dfrac{\$550,000}{\$50,000} = 11$	7 times
13. Fixed charge coverage =		
$\dfrac{\text{Income before fixed charges and taxes}}{\text{Fixed charges}}$	$\dfrac{\$600,000}{\$100,000} = 6$	5.5 times

IRWIN © a Times Mirror Higher Education Group, Inc. company. 1997

BLOCK • HIRT
Foundations
of Financial
Management
EIGHTH EDITION
T 3-9

Ratio analysis / Table 3-3

	Saxton Company	Industry Average	Conclusion
A. Profitability			
1. Profit Margin	5.0%	6.7%	Below average
2. Return on Assets	12.5%	10.0%	Above average due to high turnover
3. Return on Equity	20.0%	15.0%	Good due to ratios 2 and 10
B. Asset Utilization			
4. Receivables turnover	11.4	10	Good
5. Average collection period	32	36	Good
6. Inventory turnover	10.8	7	Good
7. Fixed asset turnover	5	5.4	Below average
8. Total asset turnover	2.5	1.5	Good
C. Liquidity			
9. Current ratio	2.67	2.1	Good
10. Quick Ratio	1.43	1.0	Good
D. Debt Utilization			
11. Debt to total assets	37.5%	33.0%	Slightly more debt
12. Times interest earned	11	7	Good
13. Fixed charge coverage	6	5.5	Good

IRWIN © a Times Mirror Higher Education Group, Inc. company. 1997

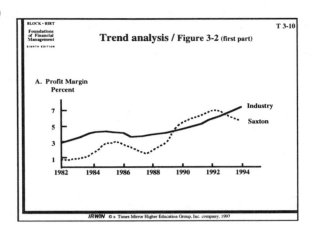

BLOCK · HIRT
Foundations
of Financial
Management
EIGHTH EDITION
T 3-10

Trend analysis / Figure 3-2 (first part)

A. Profit Margin
Percent

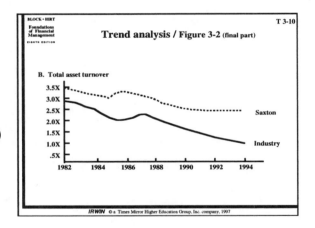

BLOCK · HIRT
Foundations
of Financial
Management
EIGHTH EDITION
T 3-10

Trend analysis / Figure 3-2 (final part)

B. Total asset turnover

BLOCK · HIRT
Foundations
of Financial
Management
EIGHTH EDITION
T 3-11

**Trend analysis in
the computer industry / Table 3-4**

	IBM		Compaq		Apple	
	Profit Margin	Return on Equity	Profit Margin	Return on Equity	Profit Margin	Return on Equity
1983	13.7%	23.6%	2.3%	2.9%	7.8%	20.3%
1984	14.3	24.8	3.9	11.8	3.9	12.7
1985	13.1	20.5	5.3	19.9	3.2	11.1
1986	9.3	13.9	6.9	23.4	8.1	22.2
1987	9.7	13.7	10.9	33.4	8.2	26.0
1988	9.8	14.7	12.0	30.5	9.8	39.9
1989	8.4	13.6	11.1	27.2	7.7	27.3
1990	8.7	14.1	12.0	23.2	8.5	32.8
1991	3.2	5.7	7.0	11.8	7.1	25.4
1992	2.2	5.2	6.1	12.4	7.5	24.2
1993	Deficit		6.5	17.7	3.6	14.1
1994	4.6	12.7	8.0	22.0	2.5	9.7
1995	8.8	25.5	7.2	21.5	3.7	12.1

BLOCK · HIRT
Foundations
of Financial
Management
EIGHTH EDITION

T 3-12

Comparison of replacement cost accounting and historical cost accounting / Table 3-7

	10 Chemical Companies		8 Drug Companies	
	Replacement Cost	Historical Cost	Replacement Cost	Historical Cost
Increase in assets	28.4%	--	15.4%	--
Decrease in net income before taxes	45.8%	--	19.3%	--
Return on assets	2.8%	6.2%	8.3%	11.4%
Return on equity	4.9%	13.5%	12.8%	19.6%
Debt-to-assets ratio	34.3%	43.8%	30.3%	35.2%
Interest coverage ratio (times interest earned)	7.1×	8.4×	15.4×	16.7×

BLOCK · HIRT
Foundations
of Financial
Management
EIGHTH EDITION

T 3-13

Table 3-8

Income Statement
For the Year 1997

	Conservative A	High Reported Income B
Sales	$ 4,000,000	$ 4,200,000
Cost of goods sold	3,000,000	2,700,000
Gross profit	1,000,000	1,500,000
Selling and administrative expense .	450,000	450,000
Operating profit	550,000	1,050,000
Interest expense	50,000	50,000
Extraordinary loss	100,000	—
Net income before taxes	400,000	1,000,000
Taxes (30%)	120,000	300,000
Net income	280,000	700,000
Extraordinary loss (net of tax) . .	—	70,000
Net income transferred to retained earnings	$ 280,000	$ 630,000

Chapter 4
Financial Forecasting

Constructing Pro Forma Statements

Pro Forma Income Statement
    Establish a Sales Projection
    Determine a Production Schedule and the Gross Profit
    Other Expense Items
    Actual Pro Forma Income Statement

Cash Budget
    Cash Receipts
    Cash Payments
    Actual Budget

Pro Forma Balance Sheet
    Explanation of Pro Forma Balance Sheet
    Analysis of Pro Forma Statement

Percent-of-Sales Method

Development of
pro forma statements / Figure 4-1

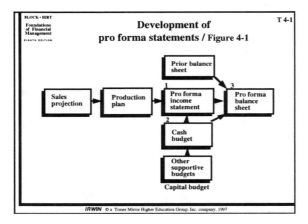

Projected wheel and caster sales
(first six months, 1997) / Table 4-1

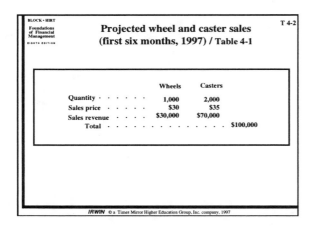

	Wheels	Casters
Quantity · · · · · ·	1,000	2,000
Sales price · · · · ·	$30	$35
Sales revenue · · · ·	$30,000	$70,000
Total · · · · · · · · · · · · · · · · ·		$100,000

BLOCK · HIRT
Foundations
of Financial
Management
EIGHTH EDITION

Stock of beginning inventory / Table 4-2 (first part)

	Wheels	Casters
Quantity . . .	85	180
Cost	$16	$20
Total value . .	$1,360	$3,600
Total		$4,960

IRWIN © a Times Mirror Higher Education Group, Inc. company. 1997

BLOCK · HIRT
Foundations
of Financial
Management
EIGHTH EDITION

Production requirements for six months / Table 4-3 (second part)

	Wheels	Casters
Projected unit sales (Table 4-1) . . .	+1,000	+2,000
Desired ending inventory (assumed to represent 10% of unit sales for the time period)	+100	+200
Beginning inventory (Table 4-2). . .	– 85	–180
Units to be produced	1,015	2,020

IRWIN © a Times Mirror Higher Education Group, Inc. company. 1997

BLOCK · HIRT
Foundations
of Financial
Management
EIGHTH EDITION

Unit costs / Table 4-4 (third part)

	Wheels	Casters
Materials	$10	$12
Labor	5	6
Overhead	3	4
Total	$18	$22

IRWIN © a Times Mirror Higher Education Group, Inc. company. 1997

BLOCK · HIRT
Foundations
of Financial
Management
EIGHTH EDITION

Total production costs / Table 4-5 (fourth part)

	Wheels	Casters	
Units to be produced (Table 4-3) . . .	1,015	2,020	
Cost per unit (Table 4-4)	$18	$22	
Total cost	$18,270	$44,440	$62,710

BLOCK · HIRT
Foundations
of Financial
Management
EIGHTH EDITION

Allocation of manufacturing costs and determination of gross profits / Table 4-6 (final part)

		Wheels	Casters	Combined
Quantity sold (Table 4-1) . .		1,000	2,000	3,000
Sales price		$30	$35	
Sales revenue		$30,000	$70,000	$100,000
Cost of goods sold:				
Old inventory (Table 4-2)				
Quantity (units) . . .	85		180	
Cost per unit . . .	$16		$20	
Total		$1,360	$3,600	
New inventory (the remainder)				
Quantity (units) . . .	915		1,820	
Cost per unit (Table 4-4)	$18		$22	
Total		16,470	40,040	
Total cost of goods sold .		17,830	43,640	$61,470
Gross profit		$12,170	$26,360	$38,530

BLOCK · HIRT
Foundations
of Financial
Management
EIGHTH EDITION

Table 4-8

Pro Forma Income Statement
June 30, 1997

Sales revenue	$100,000
Cost of goods sold	61,470
Gross profit	38,530
General and administrative expense . .	12,000
Operating profit (EBIT)	26,530
Interest expense	1,500
Earnings before taxes (EBT)	25,030
Taxes (20%)*	5,006
Earnings after taxes (EAT)	20,024
Common stock dividends	1,500
Increase in retained earnings. . . .	$ 18,524

*20 percent is applied for simplicity.

BLOCK · HIRT

Foundations
of Financial
Management

EIGHTH EDITION

T 4-5

Monthly sales
pattern / Table 4-9 (first part)

January	February	March	April	May	June
$15,000	$10,000	$15,000	$25,000	$15,000	$20,000

BLOCK · HIRT

Foundations
of Financial
Management

EIGHTH EDITION

T 4-5

Monthly cash
receipts / Table 4-10 (final part)

	December	January	February
Sales	$12,000	$15,000	$10,000
Collections:			
(20% of current sales) . .		$ 3,000	$ 2,000
Collections:			
(80% of previous			
month's sales)		9,600	12,000
Total cash receipts . .		$12,600	$14,000

	March	April	May	June
Sales	$15,000	$25,000	$15,000	$20,000
Collections:				
(20% of current sales) . .	$ 3,000	$ 5,000	$ 3,000	$ 4,000
Collections:				
(80% of previous				
month's sales	8,000	12,000	20,000	12,000
Total cash receipts . .	$11,000	$17,000	$23,000	$16,000

BLOCK · HIRT

Foundations
of Financial
Management

EIGHTH EDITION

T 4-6

Component costs of
manufactured goods / Table 4-11 (first part)

	Wheels		
	Units Produced	Cost per Unit	Total Cost
Materials . . .	1,015	$10	$10,150
Labor	1,015	5	5,075
Overhead . . .	1,015	3	3,045

	Casters			
	Units Produced	Cost per Unit	Total Cost	Combined Cost
Materials . . .	2,020	$12	$24,240	$34,390
Labor	2,020	6	12,120	17,195
Overhead . . .	2,020	4	8,080	11,125
				$62,710

Average monthly manufacturing costs /
Table 4-12 (second part)

	Total Costs	Time Frame	Average Monthly Cost
Materials . . .	$34,390	6 months	$5,732
Labor . . .	17,195	6 months	2,866
Overhead . . .	11,125	6 months	1,854

Summary of all monthly cash payments /
Table 4-13 (third part)

	December	January	February
From Table 4-12:			
Monthly material purchase. .	$4,500	$ 5,732	$ 5,732
Payment for material			
(prior month's purchase). .		$ 4,500	$ 5,732
Monthly labor cost		2,866	2,866
Monthly overhead		1,854	1,854
From Table 4-8:			
General and administrative			
expense ($12,000 over			
6 months)		2,000	2,000
Interest expense			
Taxes (two equal payments) .			
Cash dividend			
Also:			
New equipment purchases . .			8,000
Total payments		$11,220	$20,452

Summary of all monthly cash payments /
Table 4-13 (final part)

	March	April	May	June
From Table 4-12:				
Monthly material purchase . .	$ 5,732	$ 5,732	$ 5,732	$ 5,732
Payment for material				
(prior month's purchase) . .	$ 5,732	$ 5,732	$ 5,732	$ 5,732
Monthly labor cost	2,866	2,866	2,866	2,866
Monthly overhead	1,854	1,854	1,854	1,854
From Table 4-8:				
General and administrative				
expense ($12,000 over				
6 months)	2,000	2,000	2,000	2,000
Interest expense				1,500
Taxes (two equal payments) . .	2,503			2,503
Cash dividend.				1,500
Also:				
New equipment purchases . .				10,000
Total payments	$14,955	$12,452	$12,452	$27,953

BLOCK · HIRT
Foundations
of Financial
Management
EIGHTH EDITION

Monthly cash flow / Table 4-14 (first part)

	January	February	March
Total receipts (Table 4-10) . .	$12,600	$14,000	$11,000
Total payments (Table 4-13) .	11,220	20,452	14,955
Net cash flow	$ 1,380	($ 6,452)	($ 3,955)

	April	May	June
Total receipts (Table 4-10) . .	$17,000	$23,000	$16,000
Total payments (Table 4-13) .	12,452	12,452	27,953
Net cash flow	$ 4,548	$10,548	($11,953)

IRWIN © a Times Mirror Higher Education Group, Inc. company. 1997

BLOCK · HIRT
Foundations
of Financial
Management
EIGHTH EDITION

Cash budget with borrowing and repayment / Table 4-15 (final part)

	Jan.	Feb.	March	April	May	June
1. Net cash flow	$1,380	($6,452)	($3,955)	$4,548	$10,548	($11,953)
2. Beginning cash balance . .	5,000.*	6,380	5,000	5,000	5,000	11,069
3. Cumulative cash balance. .	6,380	(72)	1,045	9,548	15,548	(884)
4. Monthly loan or (repayment)	---	5,072	3,955	(4,548)	(4,479).	5,884
5. Cumulative loan balance. .	---	5,072	9,027	4,479	---	5,884
6. Ending cash balance . . .	6,380	5,000	5,000	5,000	11,069	5,000

* We assume the Goldman Corporation has a beginning cash balance of $5,000 on January 1, 1994, and it desires a minimum monthly ending cash balance of $5,000.)

IRWIN © a Times Mirror Higher Education Group, Inc. company. 1997

BLOCK · HIRT
Foundations
of Financial
Management
EIGHTH EDITION

(Table 4-16)

Balance Sheet
December 31, 1996

Assets

Current assets:	
Cash	$ 5,000
Marketable securities	3,200
Accounts receivable	9,600
Inventory	4,960
Total	22,760
Plant and equipment.	27,740
Total assets	$50,000

Liabilities and Stockholders' Equity

Accounts payable	$ 4,500
Notes payable.	0
Long-term debt	15,000
Common stock	10,000
Retained earnings	20,000
Total liabilities and stockholders' equity	$50,000

IRWIN © a Times Mirror Higher Education Group, Inc. company. 1997

18

BLOCK · HIRT
Foundations
of Financial
Management
EIGHTH EDITION

Development of a Pro Forma Balance Sheet / Figure 4-2

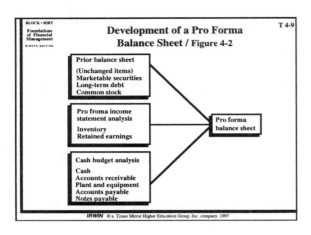

Prior balance sheet

(Unchanged items)
Marketable securities
Long-term debt
Common stock

Pro froma income statement analysis

Inventory
Retained earnings

Cash budget analysis

Cash
Accounts receivable
Plant and equipment
Accounts payable
Notes payable

Pro forma balance sheet

IRWIN © a Times Mirror Higher Education Group, Inc. company, 1997

BLOCK · HIRT
Foundations
of Financial
Management
EIGHTH EDITION

(Table 4-17)

Pro Forma Balance Sheet
June 30, 1997
Assets

Current assets:

1. Cash	$ 5,000
2. Marketable securities	3,200
3. Accounts receivable.	16,000
4. Inventory.	6,200
Total current assets	30,400
5. Plant and equipment	45,740
Total assets	$76,140

Liabilities and Stockholders' Equity

6. Accounts payable	$ 5,732
7. Notes payable	5,884
8. Long-term debt	15,000
9. Common stock.	10,500
10. Retained earnings.	39,024
Total liabilities and stockholders' equity.	$76,140

IRWIN © a Times Mirror Higher Education Group, Inc. company, 1997

BLOCK · HIRT
Foundations
of Financial
Management
EIGHTH EDITION

Table 4-18

HOWARD CORPORATION
Balance Sheet and Percent-of-Sales Table

Assets		Liabilities and Stockholders' Equity	
Cash	$ 5,000	Accounts payable	$ 40,000
Accounts receivable	40,000	Accrued expenses	10,000
Inventory.	25,000	Notes payable	15,000
Total current assets	70,000	Common stock	10,000
Equipment	50,000	Retained earnings	45,000
Total assets	$120,000	Total liabilities and stockholders' equity	$120,000

$200,000 sales

Percent of Sales

Cash	2.5%	Accounts payable	20.0%
Accounts receivable	20.0	Accrued expenses	5.0
Inventory.	12.5		
Total current assets	35.0		
Equipment	25.0		
	60.0%		

IRWIN © a Times Mirror Higher Education Group, Inc. company, 1997

BLOCK • HIRT
Foundations
of Financial
Management
EIGHTH EDITION
T -CH5

Chapter 5
Operating and Financial Leverage

Leverage in a Business

Operating Leverage
    Break-even Analysis
    A More Conservative Approach
    The Risk Factor
    Cash Break-Even Analysis
    Degree of Operating Leverage
    Limitations of Analysis

Financial Leverage
    Impact on Earnings
    Degree of Financial Leverage
    Limitations to Use of Financial Leverage

Combining Operating and Financial Leverage
    Degree of Combined Leverage
    A Word of Caution

BLOCK • HIRT
Foundations
of Financial
Management
EIGHTH EDITION
T 5-1

Break-even chart: Leveraged firm /
Figure 5-1

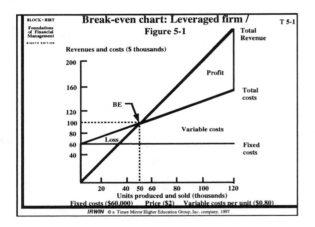

Revenues and costs ($ thousands)

Total Revenue

Profit

Total costs

BE

Variable costs

Loss

Fixed costs

200
160
120
100
80
60
40

20 40 50 60 80 100 120
Units produced and sold (thousands)

Fixed costs ($60,000)   Price ($2)   Variable costs per unit ($0.80)

BLOCK • HIRT
Foundations
of Financial
Management
EIGHTH EDITION
T 5-2

Volume-cost-profit analysis:
Leveraged firm / Table 5-2

Units Sold	Total Variable Costs	Fixed Costs	Total Costs	Total Revenue	Operating Income (loss)
0	0	$ 60,000	$ 60,000	0	$(60,000)
20,000	$16,000	60,000	76,000	$ 40,000	(36,000)
40,000	32,000	60,000	92,000	80,000	(12,000)
50,000	40,000	60,000	100,000	100,000	0
60,000	48,000	60,000	108,000	120,000	12,000
80,000	64,000	60,000	124,000	160,000	36,000
100,000	80,000	60,000	140,000	200,000	60,000

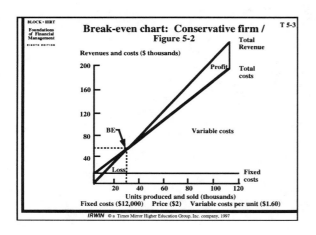

Break-even chart: Conservative firm /
Figure 5-2

T 5-3

BLOCK • HIRT
Foundations
of Financial
Management
EIGHTH EDITION

Revenues and costs ($ thousands)

Total
Revenue

Profit   Total
costs

Variable costs

BE

Loss

Fixed
costs

Units produced and sold (thousands)
Fixed costs ($12,000)   Price ($2)   Variable costs per unit ($1.60)

IRWIN © a Times Mirror Higher Education Group, Inc. company, 1997

BLOCK • HIRT
Foundations
of Financial
Management
EIGHTH EDITION

Volume-cost-profit analysis:
Conservative firm / Table 5-3

Units Sold	Total Variable Costs	Fixed Costs	Total Costs	Total Revenue	Operating Income (loss)
0	0	$ 12,000	$ 12,000	0	$ (12,000)
20,000	$32,000	12,000	44,000	$ 40,000	(4,000)
30,000	48,000	12,000	60,000	60,000	0
40,000	64,000	12,000	76,000	80,000	4,000
60,000	96,000	12,000	108,000	120,000	12,000
80,000	128,000	12,000	140,000	160,000	20,000
100,000	160,000	12,000	172,000	200,000	28,000

IRWIN © a Times Mirror Higher Education Group, Inc. company, 1997

BLOCK • HIRT
Foundations
of Financial
Management
EIGHTH EDITION

Operating income or loss / Table 5-4

Units		Leveraged Firm (Table 5-2)	Conservative Firm (Table 5-3)
0	. . .	$(60,000)	$(12,000)
20,000	. . .	(36,000)	(4,000)
40,000	. . .	(12,000)	4,000
60,000	. . .	12,000	12,000
80,000	. . .	36,000	20,000
100,000	. . .	60,000	28,000

IRWIN © a Times Mirror Higher Education Group, Inc. company, 1997

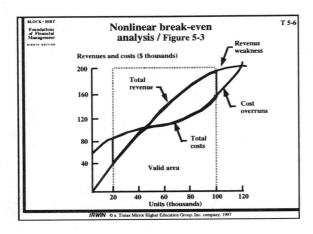

Nonlinear break-even analysis / Figure 5-3

T 5-6

BLOCK • HIRT
Foundations of Financial Management
EIGHTH EDITION

Revenues and costs ($ thousands)

Revenue weakness

Total revenue

Cost overruns

Total costs

Valid area

Units (thousands)

IRWIN © a Times Mirror Higher Education Group, Inc. company. 1997

BLOCK • HIRT
Foundations of Financial Management
EIGHTH EDITION

Impact of financing plan on earnings per share / Table 5-5 (first part)

	Plan A (leveraged)	Plan B (conservative)
1. EBIT (0)		
Earnings before interest and taxes (EBIT)	0	0
— Interest (I)	$(12,000)	$ (4,000)
Earnings before taxes (EBT)	(12,000)	(4,000)
— Taxes (T) *	(6,000)	(2,000)
Earnings after taxes (EAT)	$ (6,000)	$ (2,000)
Shares	8,000	24,000
Earnings per share (EPS)	$ (0.75)	$ (0.08)
2. EBIT ($12,000)		
Earnings before interest and taxes (EBIT)	$12,000	$12,000
— Interest (I)	12,000	4,000
Earnings before taxes (EBT)	0	8,000
— Taxes (T)	0	4,000
Earnings after taxes (EAT)	$ 0	$ 4,000
Shares	8,000	24,000
Earnings per share (EPS)	0	$0.17

* The assumption is that large losses can be written off against other income, perhaps in other years, thus providing the firm with a tax savings benefit. The tax rate is 50 percent for ease of computation.

IRWIN © a Times Mirror Higher Education Group, Inc. company. 1997

BLOCK • HIRT
Foundations of Financial Management
EIGHTH EDITION

Impact of financing plan on earnings per share / Table 5-5 (second part)

	Plan A (leveraged)	Plan B (conservative)
3. EBIT ($16,000)		
Earnings before interest and taxes (EBIT)	$ 16,000	$ 16,000
— Interest (I)	12,000	4,000
Earnings before taxes (EBT)	4,000	12,000
— Taxes (T)	2,000	6,000
Earnings after taxes (EAT)	$ 2,000	$ 6,000
Shares	8,000	24,000
Earnings per share (EPS)	$0.25	$0.25
4. EBIT ($36,000)		
Earnings before interest and taxes (EBIT)	$ 36,000	$ 36,000
— Interest (I)	12,000	4,000
Earnings before taxes (EBT)	24,000	32,000
— Taxes (T)	12,000	16,000
Earnings after taxes (EAT)	$ 12,000	$ 16,000
Shares	8,000	24,000
Earnings per share (EPS)	$1.50	$0.67

IRWIN © a Times Mirror Higher Education Group, Inc. company. 1997

Impact of financing plan
on earnings per share / Table 5-5 (final part)

	Plan A (leveraged)	Plan B (conservative)
5. EBIT ($60,000)		
Earnings before interest and taxes (EBIT)	$ 60,000	$ 60,000
— Interest (I)	12,000	4,000
Earnings before taxes (EBT)	48,000	56,000
— Taxes (T)	24,000	28,000
Earnings after taxes (EAT)	$ 24,000	$ 28,000
Shares	8,000	24,000
Earnings per share (EPS)	$3.00	$ 1.17

Financing plans and
earnings per share / Figure 5-4

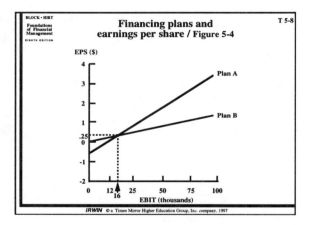

Income statement / Table 5-6

Sales (total revenue) (80,000 units @ $2)	$160,000	Operating leverage
— Fixed costs	60,000	
— Variable costs ($0.80 per unit)	64,000	
Operating income	$ 36,000	
Earnings before interest and taxes	$ 36,000	Financial leverage
— Interest	12,000	
Earnings before taxes	24,000	
— Taxes	12,000	
Earnings after taxes	$ 12,000	
Shares	8,000	
Earnings per share	$1.50	

23

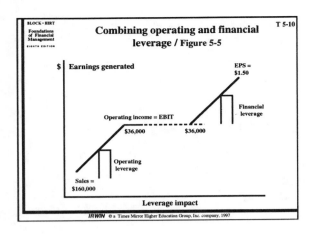

BLOCK · HIRT
Foundations
of Financial
Management
EIGHTH EDITION

Combining operating and financial leverage / Figure 5-5

$ | Earnings generated

EPS = $1.50

Operating income = EBIT

$36,000 $36,000

Financial leverage

Operating leverage

Sales = $160,000

Leverage impact

IRWIN © a Times Mirror Higher Education Group, Inc. company, 1997

BLOCK · HIRT
Foundations
of Financial
Management
EIGHTH EDITION

Operating and financial leverage / Table 5-7

	(Taken from Table 5-6)		
Sales — $2 per unit (80,000 units)	$160,000	(100,000 units)	$200,000
— Fixed costs	60,000		60,000
— Variable costs ($0.80 per unit)	64,000		80,000
Operating income (EBIT)	36,000		60,000
— Interest	12,000		12,000
Earnings before taxes	24,000		48,000
— Taxes	12,000		24,000
Earnings after taxes	$ 12,000		$ 24,000
Shares	8,000		8,000
Earnings per share	$1.50		$3.00

IRWIN © a Times Mirror Higher Education Group, Inc. company, 1997

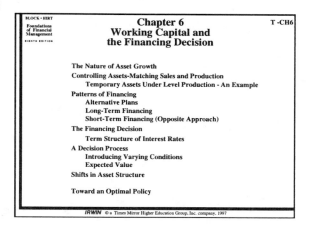

Chapter 6
Working Capital and
the Financing Decision

T -CH6

The Nature of Asset Growth
Controlling Assets-Matching Sales and Production
    Temporary Assets Under Level Production - An Example
Patterns of Financing
    Alternative Plans
    Long-Term Financing
    Short-Term Financing (Opposite Approach)
The Financing Decision
    Term Structure of Interest Rates
A Decision Process
    Introducing Varying Conditions
    Expected Value
Shifts in Asset Structure

Toward an Optimal Policy

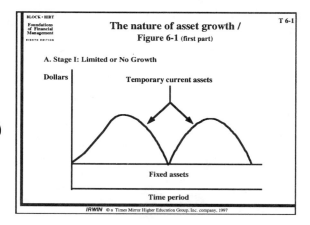

The nature of asset growth /
Figure 6-1 (first part)

T 6-1

A. Stage I: Limited or No Growth

Dollars

Temporary current assets

Fixed assets

Time period

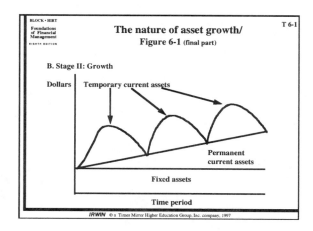

The nature of asset growth/
Figure 6-1 (final part)

T 6-1

B. Stage II: Growth

Dollars

Temporary current assets

Permanent
current assets

Fixed assets

Time period

Yawakuzi sales forecast
(in units) / Table 6-1

1st Quarter		2nd Quarter		3rd Quarter		4th Quarter	
October	300	January	0	April	1,000	July	2,000
November	150	February	0	May	2,000	August	1,000
December	50	March	600	June	2,000	September	500

Total sales of 9,600 units at $3,000 each = $28,800,000 in sales.

Yawakuzi's production schedule and inventory / Table 6-2

	Beginning inventory	+	Production (level production)	–	Sales	=	Ending inventory	Inventory (at cost of $2,000 per unit)
October	800		800		300		1,300	$2,600,000
November	1,300		800		150		1,950	3,900,000
December	1,950		800		50		2,700	5,400,000
January	2,700		800		0		3,500	7,000,000
February	3,500		800		0		4,300	8,600,000
March	4,300		800		600		4,500	9,000,000
April	4,500		800		1,000		4,300	8,600,000
May	4,300		800		2,000		3,100	6,200,000
June	3,100		800		2,000		1,900	3,800,000
July	1,900		800		2,000		700	1,400,000
August	700		800		1,000		500	1,000,000
September	500		800		500		800	1,600,000

Sales forecast, cash receipts and payments, and cash budget / Table 6-3 (first part)

	Oct	Nov	Dec	Jan	Feb	Mar	Apr	May	June	July	Aug	Sept
Sales Forecast ($ millions)												
Sales (units)	300	150	50	0	0	600	1,000	2,000	2,000	2,000	1,000	500
Sales (unit price, $3,000)	$0.9	$0.45	$0.15	$0	$0	$1.8	$3.0	$6.0	$6.0	$6.0	$3.0	$1.5
Cash Receipts Schedule ($ millions)												
50% cash	$.45	$.225	$.075	$0	$0	$.9	$1.5	$3.0	$3.0	$3.0	$1.5	$.75
50% cash from prior month's sales	.75*	.450	.225	.075	0	0	.9	1.5	3.0	3.0	3.0	1.5
Total cash receipts	$1.20	$.675	$.300	$.075	0	$.9	$2.4	$4.5	$6.0	$6.0	$4.5	$2.25

*Assumes September sales of $1.5 million.

Sales forecast, cash receipts and payments, and cash budget / Table 6-3 (final part)

T 6-4

	Oct	Nov	Dec	Jan	Feb	Mar	Apr	May	June	July	Aug	Sept
				Cash Payments Schedule ($ millions)								
Constant production of $2,000 per unit	$1.6	$1.6	$1.6	$1.6	$1.6	$1.6	$1.6	$1.6	$1.6	$1.6	$1.6	$1.6
Overhead	.4	.4	.4	.4	.4	.4	.4	.4	.4	.4	.4	.4
Dividends and interest	–	–	–	–	–	–	–	–	–	–	1.0	–
Taxes	.3			.3			.3			.3		
Total cash payments	$2.3	$2.0	$2.0	$2.3	$2.0	$2.0	$2.3	$2.0	$2.0	$2.3	$3.0	$2.0

Cash Budget ($ millions; required minimum balance is $.25 million)

	Oct	Nov	Dec	Jan	Feb	Mar	Apr	May	June	July	Aug	Sept
Cash flow	$(1.1)	$(1.325)	$(1.7)	$(2.225)	$(2.0)	$(1.1)	$.1	$2.5	$4.0	$3.7	$1.5	$.25
Beginning cash	.25†	.25	.25	.25	.25	.25	.25	.25	.25	.25	1.1	2.60
Cumulative cash balance	$(.85)	$(1.075)	$(1.45)	$(1.975)	$(1.75)	$(.85)	$.35	$2.75	$4.25	$3.95	$2.6	$2.85
Monthly loan or (repayment)	1.1	1.325	1.7	2.225	2.0	1.1	(0.1)	(2.5)	(4.0)	(2.85)	0	0
Cumulative loan	1.1	2.425	4.125	6.350	8.35	9.45	9.35	6.85	2.85	0	0	0
Ending cash balance	.25	.25	.25	.25	.25	.25	.25	.25	.25	1.1	2.6	2.85

†Assumes cash balance of $.25 million at the beginning of October and that this is the desired minimum cash balance.

Total current assets, first year ($ millions) / Table 6-4

T 6-5

	Cash	Accounts Receivable	Inventory	Total Current Assets
October	$0.25	$0.450	$2.6	$3.30
November	0.25	0.225	3.9	4.375
December	0.25	0.075	5.4	5.725
January	0.25	0.00	7.0	7.25
February	0.25	0.00	8.6	8.85
March	0.25	0.90	9.0	10.15
April	0.25	1.50	8.6	10.35
May	0.25	3.00	6.2	9.45
June	0.25	3.00	3.8	7.05
July	1.10	3.00	1.4	5.50
August	2.60	1.50	1.0	5.10
September	2.85	0.75	1.6	5.20

Cash budget and assets for second year with no growth in sales ($ millions) / Table 6-5 (first part)

T 6-6

	End of First Year	Second Year											
	Sept	Oct	Nov	Dec	Jan	Feb	Mar	Apr	May	June	July	Aug	Sept
Cash flow	$0.25	$(1.1)	$(1.325)	$(1.7)	$(2.225)	$(2.0)	$(1.1)	$0.1	$2.5	$4.0	$3.7	$1.5	$0.25
Beginning cash	2.60	2.85	1.750	0.425	0.25	0.25	0.25	0.25	0.25	0.25	0.25	3.7	5.2
Cumulative cash balance		1.75	0.425	(1.275)	(1.975)	(1.75)	(0.85)	0.35	2.75	4.25	3.95	5.2	5.45
Monthly loan or (repayment)		–	–	1.525	2.225	2.0	1.1	(0.1)	(2.5)	(4.0)	(0.25)	–	–
Cumulative loan		–	–	1.525	3.750	5.75	6.85	6.75	4.25	0.25	0.	–	–
Ending cash balance	$2.85	$1.75	$0.425	$0.25	$0.25	$0.25	$0.25	$0.25	$0.25	$0.25	$3.70	$5.2	$5.45

Cash budget and assets for second year with no growth in sales ($ millions) /Table 6-5 (final part)

T 6-6

	End of First Year	Second Year											
	Sept	Oct	Nov	Dec	Jan	Feb	Mar	Apr	May	June	July	Aug	Sept
						Total Current Assets							
Ending cash balance	$2.85	$1.75	$0.425	$0.25	$0.25	$0.25	$0.25	$0.25	$0.25	$0.25	$3.70	$5.2	$5.45
Accounts receivable	0.75	0.45	0.225	0.075	0.	0.	0.95	1.50	3.0	3.0	3.0	1.5	0.75
Inventory	1.6	2.6	3.9	5.4	7.0	8.6	9.0	8.6	6.2	3.8	1.4	1.0	1.60
Total current assets	$5.2	$4.8	$4.55	$5.725	$7.25	$8.85	$10.15	$10.35	$9.45	$7.05	$8.1	$7.7	$7.80

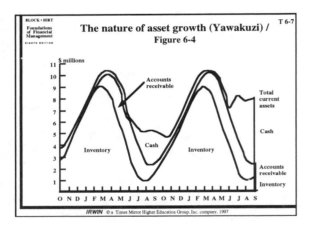

The nature of asset growth (Yawakuzi) / Figure 6-4

T 6-7

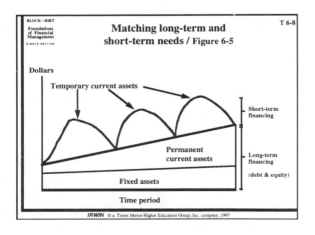

Matching long-term and short-term needs / Figure 6-5

T 6-8

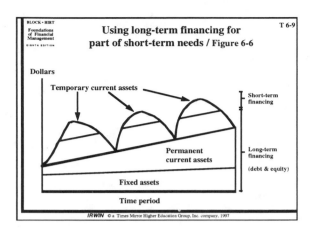

Using long-term financing for part of short-term needs / Figure 6-6

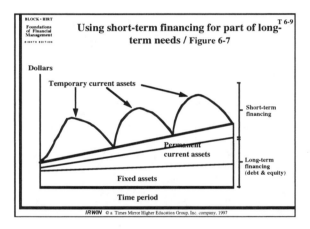

Using short-term financing for part of long-term needs / Figure 6-7

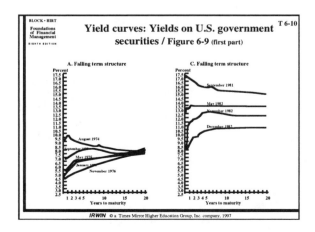

Yield curves: Yields on U.S. government securities / Figure 6-9 (first part)

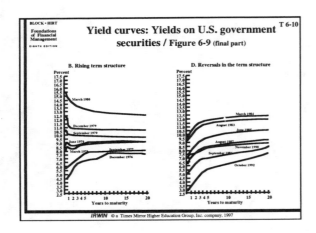

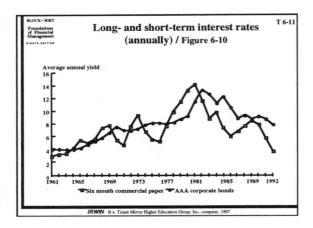

T 6-12a

Alternative financing plans /
Table 6-7

EDWARDS CORPORATION

	Plan A	Plan B
Part 1. Current assets		
Temporary	$250,000	$250,000
Permanent	250,000	250,000
Total current assets . . .	500,000	500,000
Short-term financing (6%) . .	500,000	150,000
Long-term financing (10%) .	0	350,000
	$500,000	$500,000
Part 2. Fixed assets	$100,000	$100,000
Long-term financing (10%) .	$100,000	$100,000
Part 3. Total financing (summary of parts 1 & 2)		
Short-term (6%)	$500,000	$150,000
Long-term (10%	100,000	450,000
	$600,000	$600,000

BLOCK · HIRT
Foundations
of Financial
Management
EIGHTH EDITION
T 6-12b

Impact of financing plans on earnings / Table 6-8

EDWARDS CORPORATION

Plan A

Earnings before interest and taxes	$200,000
Interest (short-term), 6% × $500,000	− 30,000
Interest (long-term), 10% × $100,000	− 10,000
Earnings before taxes	160,000
Taxes (50%)	80,000
Earnings after taxes	$ 80,000

Plan B

Earnings before interest and taxes	$200,000
Interest (short-term), 6% × $150,000	− 9,000
Interest (long-term), 10% × $450,000	− 45,000
Earnings before taxes	146,000
Taxes (50%)	73,000
Earnings after taxes	$ 73,000

IRWIN © a Times Mirror Higher Education Group, Inc. company, 1997

BLOCK · HIRT
Foundations
of Financial
Management
EIGHTH EDITION
T 6-13

Expected returns under different economic conditions / Table 6-9 (first part)

EDWARDS CORPORATION

1. Normal conditions	Expected higher return under Plan A	Probability of normal conditions		Expected outcome	
	$7,000	×	.80	=	+$5,600
2. Tight money	Expected lower return under Plan A	Probability of tight money			
	($15,000)	×	.20	=	(3,000)
Expected value of return for Plan A versus Plan B				=	+$2,600

IRWIN © a Times Mirror Higher Education Group, Inc. company, 1997

BLOCK · HIRT
Foundations
of Financial
Management
EIGHTH EDITION
T 6-13

Expected returns for high-risk firm / Table 6-10 (final part)

1. Normal conditions	Expected higher return under Plan A	Probability of normal conditions		Expected outcome	
	$7,000	×	.80	=	+$5,600
2. Tight money	Expected lower return under Plan A	Probability of tight money			
	($50,000)	×	.20	=	(10,000)
Negative expected value of return for Plan A versus Plan B				=	($4,400)

IRWIN © a Times Mirror Higher Education Group, Inc. company, 1997

BLOCK • HIRT

Foundations
of Financial
Management

EIGHTH EDITION

Asset liquidity and financing assets /Table 6-11

Financing Plan	Asset Liquidity	
	Low Liquidity	High Liquidity
Short-term	1 High Profit High risk	2 Moderate profit Moderate risk
Long-term	3 Moderate profit Moderate risk	4 Low profit Low risk

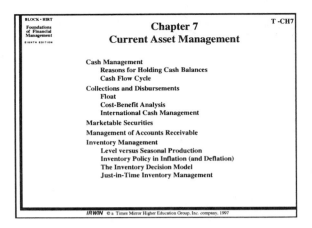

Foundations of Financial Management
EIGHTH EDITION

T -CH7

Chapter 7
Current Asset Management

Cash Management
    Reasons for Holding Cash Balances
    Cash Flow Cycle
Collections and Disbursements
    Float
    Cost-Benefit Analysis
    International Cash Management
Marketable Securities
Management of Accounts Receivable
Inventory Management
    Level versus Seasonal Production
    Inventory Policy in Inflation (and Deflation)
    The Inventory Decision Model
    Just-in-Time Inventory Management

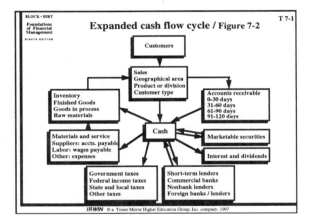

Expanded cash flow cycle / Figure 7-2

T 7-1

Customers

Sales
Geographical area
Product or division
Customer type

Inventory
Finished Goods
Goods in process
Raw materials

Accounts receivable
0-30 days
31-60 days
61-90 days
91-120 days

Cash

Marketable securities

Materials and service
Suppliers: accts. payable
Labor: wages payable
Other: expenses

Interest and dividends

Government taxes
Federal income taxes
State and local taxes
Other taxes

Short-term lenders
Commercial banks
Nonbank lenders
Foreign banks / lenders

BLOCK · HIRT
Foundations of Financial Management
EIGHTH EDITION

T 7-2

The use of float to provide funds /
Table 7-1 (first part)

	Corporate Books	Bank Books (usable funds) (amounts actually cleared)
Initial amount	$ 100,000	$ 100,000
Deposits	+ 1,000,000	+ 800,000
Checks	− 900,000	− 400,000
Balance	+ $ 200,000	+ $ 500,000
	+ $300,000 float	

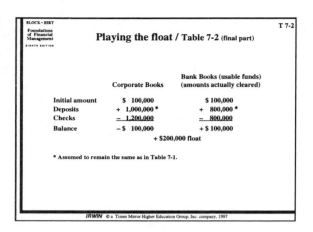

BLOCK · HIRT

Foundations
of Financial
Management

EIGHTH EDITION

T 7-2

Playing the float / Table 7-2 (final part)

	Corporate Books	Bank Books (usable funds) (amounts actually cleared)
Initial amount	$ 100,000	$ 100,000
Deposits	+ 1,000,000 *	+ 800,000 *
Checks	− 1,200,000	− 800,000
Balance	− $ 100,000	+ $ 100,000
	+ $200,000 float	

* Assumed to remain the same as in Table 7-1.

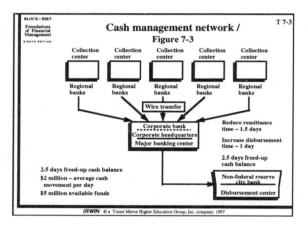

BLOCK · HIRT

Foundations
of Financial
Management

EIGHTH EDITION

T 7-3

Cash management network /
Figure 7-3

Collection center — Collection center — Collection center — Collection center — Collection center

Regional banks — Regional banks — Regional banks — Regional banks — Regional banks

Wire transfer

Corporate bank
Corporate headquarters
Major banking center

Reduce remittance time − 1.5 days

Increase disbursement time − 1 day

2.5 days freed-up cash balance

2.5 days freed-up cash balance
$2 million − average cash movement per day
$5 million available funds

Non-federal reserve city bank
Disbursement center

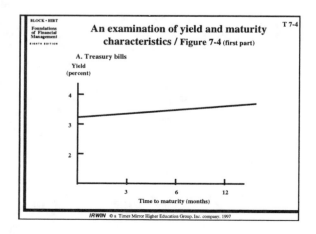

BLOCK · HIRT

Foundations
of Financial
Management

EIGHTH EDITION

T 7-4

An examination of yield and maturity
characteristics / Figure 7-4 (first part)

A. Treasury bills

Yield (percent)

Time to maturity (months)

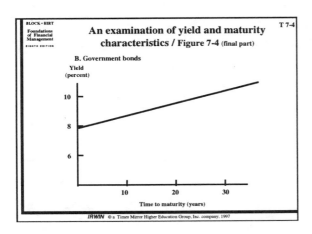

BLOCK · HIRT

Foundations
of Financial
Management

EIGHTH EDITION

T 7-4

An examination of yield and maturity characteristics / Figure 7-4 (final part)

B. Government bonds

Yield
(percent)

10

8

6

10   20   30

Time to maturity (years)

BLOCK · HIRT

Foundations
of Financial
Management

EIGHTH EDITION

T 7-5

Types of short-term investments / Table 7-3 (first part)

	Maturity*	Minimum Amount	Safety	Marketability	Yield March 22, 1980	Yield July 13, 1995
Federal government securities:						
Treasury bills	3 months	$10,000	Excellent	Excellent	14.76	5.38
Treasury bills	1 year	10,000	Excellent	Excellent	13.89	5.42
Treasury notes	1-10 years	5,000	Excellent	Excellent	13.86	5.78
Federal agency securities:						
Federal Home Loan Bank	1-10 years	5,000	Excellent	Excellent	14.40	5.84
Federal Land Bank	1-5 years	5,000	Excellent	Excellent	14.32	5.74
Nongovernment securities:						
Certificates of deposit (large)	1 month	10,000	Good	Good	16.97	5.15
Certificates of deposit (small)	90 days	500	Good	Poor	15.90	5.78
Commercial paper	3 months	25,000	Good	Fair	17.40	5.73
Banker's acceptances	90 days	None	Good	Good	17.22	5.64
Eurodollar deposits	3 months	25,000	Good	Excellent	18.98	5.88
Savings accounts	Open	None	Excellent	None†	5-5.5	2.15
Money market funds	Open	500	Good	None†	14.50	5.64
Money market deposits accts. (financial institutions)	Open	1,000	Excellent	None†	–	2.83

* Several of the above securities can be purchased with maturities longer than those indicated. The above are the most commonly quoted.
† Though not marketable, these investments are still highly liquid in that funds may be withdrawn without penalty.

Source: *The Wall Street Journal*, Thursday July 13, 1995, page C19

BLOCK · HIRT

Foundations
of Financial
Management

EIGHTH EDITION

T 7-6

Trucking Industry Credit Score Report / Table 7-4 (first part)

TRUCKING INDUSTRY CREDIT SCORE REPORT
LEVEL ONE

D-U-N-S: 00-007-7743

DATE PRINTED: APR 11, 199-
BUSINESS RECORD DATE: AUG 199-

GORMAN PRINTING

492 KOLLER STREET
SAN FRANCISCO, CA 94110
TEL: 415-555-0000

SIC: 27 52

LOB: COMMERCIAL PRINTING

PAYMENTS REPORTED FROM MEMBERS OF THE TRUCKING INDUSTRY
(amounts may be rounded to nearest figure in prescribed ranges)

Payments Reported	Paying Record	High Credit	Now Owes	Past Due	Selling Terms	Last Sale Within
06/9-	Ppt	25,000	25,000	0	1 10 N30	1 mo
02/9-	Ppt	1,000	50	50		
	Slow 30	750	250	250	N15	6-12 mo
12/9-	Ppt-Slow 30	50,000	10,000	5,000	1 10 N30	1 mo

Payment experiences reflect how bills are met in relation to the terms granted. In some instances, payment beyond terms can be the result of disputes over merchandise.
Source: Dun & Bradstreet, Inc.

BLOCK · HIRT
Foundations
of Financial
Management
EIGHTH EDITION

T 7-6

Trucking Industry Credit Scoring Section /
Table 7-4 (final part)

The TRUCKING INDUSTRY CREDIT RISK SCORE predicts the likelihood of a firm paying trucking bills in a delinquent manner (90 Days Past Terms) during the next 12 months, based on the information in Dun & Bradstreet's files. The score was calculated using statistically valid models derived from D&B's extensive information files and includes analysis of the trucking industry payment information.

The PERCENTILE ranks the firm relative to all businesses who use trucking services. For example, a firm in the 80th percentile is a better risk than 79% of all trucking customers.

The INCIDENCE OF DELINQUENT PAYMENT is the proportion of trucking customers with scores in this range that were reported 90 days past due by members of the trucking industry. The incidence of delinquent payment for the entire population of trucking customers was 11.8% over the past year.

TRUCKING INDUSTRY CREDIT RISK SCORE: (1 HIGHEST RISK – 100 LOWEST RISK)	42
PERCENTILE	6
INCIDENCE OF DELINQUENT PAYMENT FOR TRUCKING CUSTOMERS WITH SCORES 41–45:	39.9%

BLOCK · HIRT
Foundations
of Financial
Management
EIGHTH EDITION

T 7-7

Determining the optimum inventory level / Figure 7-7

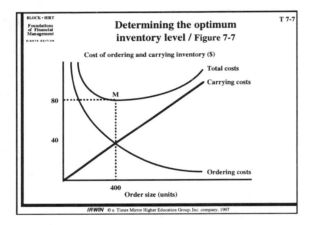

Cost of ordering and carrying inventory ($)

Total costs

Carrying costs

M

80

40

Ordering costs

400

Order size (units)

Chapter 8
Sources of Short-Term Financing

Trade Credit
    Payment Period
    Cash Discount Policy
    Net Credit Position
Bank Credit
Financing through Commercial Paper
Foreign Borrowing
Use of Collateral in Short-Term Financing
Accounts Receivable Financing
Inventory Financing
Hedging to Reduce Borrowing Risk

Movement of the Prime Rate and the London Interbank Offer Rate on U.S. Dollar Deposits / Figure 8-1

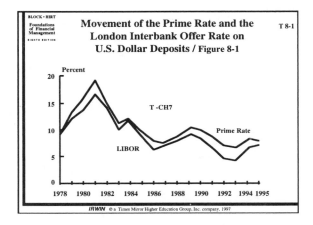

Total commercial paper outstanding / Figure 8-2

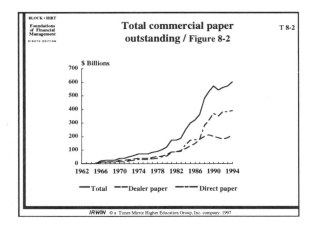

BLOCK · HIRT
Foundations
of Financial
Management
EIGHTH EDITION

T - CH9

Chapter 9
The Time Value of Money

Relationship to the Capital Outlay Decision

Future Value - Single Amount

Present Value - Single Amount

Future Value - Annuity

Present Value - Annuity

Graphical Presentation of Time Value Relationships

Determining the Annuity Value

Determining the Yield on an Investment

Special Consideration in Time Value Analysis

BLOCK · HIRT
Foundations
of Financial
Management
EIGHTH EDITION

T 9-1

Future value of \$1 (FV_{IF}) / Table 9-1

Periods	1%	2%	3%	4%	6%	8%	10%
1....	1.010	1.020	1.030	1.040	1.060	1.080	1.100
2....	1.020	1.040	1.061	1.082	1.124	1.166	1.210
3....	1.030	1.061	1.093	1.125	1.191	1.260	1.331
4....	1.041	1.082	1.126	1.170	1.262	1.360	1.464
5....	1.051	1.104	1.159	1.217	1.338	1.469	1.611
10....	1.105	1.219	1.344	1.480	1.791	2.159	2.594
20....	1.220	1.486	1.806	2.191	3.207	4.661	6.727

BLOCK · HIRT
Foundations
of Financial
Management
EIGHTH EDITION

T 9-2

Relationship of present value and future value / Figure 9-1

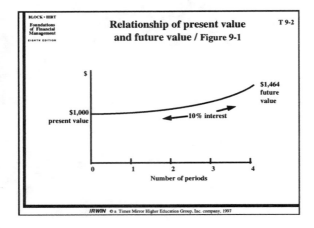

T 9-3

Present value of $1 ($PV_{IF}$) / Table 9-2

Periods	1%	2%	3%	4%	6%	8%	10%
1	0.990	0.980	0.971	0.962	0.943	0.926	0.909
2	0.980	0.961	0.943	0.925	0.890	0.857	0.826
3	0.971	0.942	0.915	0.889	0.840	0.794	0.751
4	0.961	0.924	0.888	0.855	0.792	0.735	0.683
5	0.951	0.906	0.863	0.822	0.747	0.681	0.621
10	0.905	0.820	0.744	0.676	0.558	0.463	0.386
20	0.820	0.673	0.554	0.456	0.312	0.215	0.149

An expanded table is presented in Appendix B

T 9-4

Compounding process for annuity /Figure 9-2

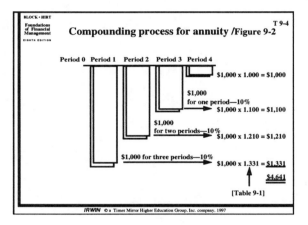

Period 0   Period 1   Period 2   Period 3   Period 4

$1,000 x 1.000 = $1,000

$1,000
for one period—10%
$1,000 x 1.100 = $1,100

$1,000
for two periods—10%
$1,000 x 1.210 = $1,210

$1,000 for three periods—10%
$1,000 x 1.331 = $1,331

$4,641

[Table 9-1]

T 9-5

Future value of an annuity of $1 ($FV_{IFA}$) / Table 9-3

Periods	1%	2%	3%	4%	6%	8%	10%
1	1.000	1.000	1.000	1.000	1.000	1.000	1.000
2	2.010	2.020	2.030	2.040	2.060	2.080	2.100
3	3.030	3.060	3.091	3.122	3.184	3.246	3.310
4	4.060	4.122	4.184	4.246	4.375	4.506	4.641
5	5.101	5.204	5.309	5.416	5.637	5.867	6.105
10	10.462	10.950	11.464	12.006	13.181	14.487	15.937
20	22.019	24.297	26.870	29.778	36.786	45.762	57.275
30	34.785	40.588	47.575	56.085	79.058	113.280	164.490

An expanded table is presented in Appendix C

BLOCK · HIRT
Foundations
of Financial
Management
EIGHTH EDITION

T 9-6

Present value of an annuity of $1 (PV$_{IFA}$) /
Table 9-4

Periods	1%	2%	3%	4%	6%	8%	10%
1	0.990	0.980	0.971	0.962	0.943	0.926	0.909
2	1.970	1.942	1.913	1.886	1.833	1.783	1.736
3	2.941	2.884	2.829	2.775	2.673	2.577	2.487
4	3.902	3.808	3.717	3.630	3.465	3.312	3.170
5	4.853	4.713	4.580	4.452	4.212	3.993	3.791
8	7.652	7.325	7.020	6.773	6.210	5.747	5.335
10	9.471	8.983	8.530	8.111	7.360	6.710	6.145
20	18.046	16.351	14.877	13.590	11.470	9.818	8.514
30	25.808	22.396	19.600	17.292	13.765	11.258	9.427

An expanded table is presented in Appendix D

IRWIN © a Times Mirror Higher Education Group, Inc. company, 1997

sLOCK · HIRT
Foundations
of Financial
Management
EIGHTH EDITION

T 9-7

Relationship of present value
to annuity / Table 9-5

Year	Beginning Balance	Annual Interest (6 percent)	Annual Withdrawal	Ending Balance
1	$10,000.00	$600.00	$2,886.00	$7,714.00
2	7,714.00	462.84	2,886.00	5,290.84
3	5,290.84	317.45	2,886.00	2,722.29
4	2,722.29	163.71	2,886.00	0

IRWIN © a Times Mirror Higher Education Group, Inc. company, 1997

BLOCK · HIRT
Foundations
of Financial
Management
EIGHTH EDITION

T 9-8

Payoff table for loan
(amortization table) / Table 9-6

Period	Beginning Balance	Annual Payment	Annual Interest Withdrawal	Repayment on Principal	Ending Balance
1	$40,000	$4,074	$3,200	$ 874	$39,126
2	39,126	4,074	3,130	944	38,182
3	38,182	4,074	3,055	1,019	37,163

IRWIN © a Times Mirror Higher Education Group, Inc. company, 1997

Determining the yield on an investment

		Formula	Table	Appendix
Future value – single amount	(9-1)	$FV = PV \times FV_{IF}$	9-1	A
Present value – single amount	(9-2)	$PV = FV \times PV_{IF}$	9-2	B
Future value – annuity	(9-3)	$FV_A = A \times FV_{IFA}$	9-3	C
Present value – annuity	(9-4)	$PV_A = A \times PV_{IFA}$	9-4	D
Annuity equaling a future value	(9-5)	$A = \dfrac{FV_A}{FV_{IFA}}$	9-3	C
Annuity equaling a present value	(9-6)	$A = \dfrac{PV_A}{PV_{IFA}}$	9-4	D

Finding present value (first part)

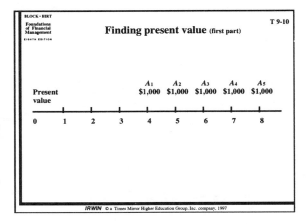

Finding present value (second part)

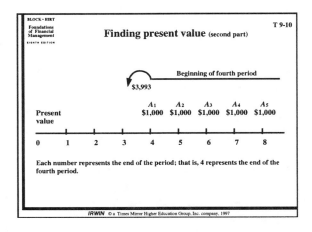

Each number represents the end of the period; that is, 4 represents the end of the fourth period.

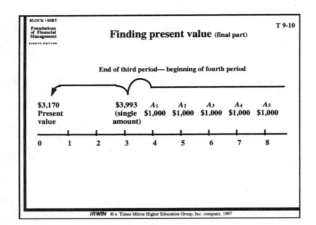

BLOCK · HIRT
Foundations
of Financial
Management
EIGHTH EDITION

T 9-10

Finding present value (final part)

End of third period— beginning of fourth period

| $3,170 Present value | | | $3,993 (single amount) | A_1 $1,000 | A_2 $1,000 | A_3 $1,000 | A_4 $1,000 | A_5 $1,000 |

0   1   2   3   4   5   6   7   8

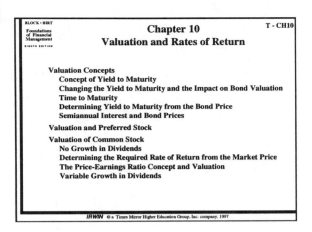

BLOCK • HIRT

Foundations
of Financial
Management

EIGHTH EDITION

T - CH10

Chapter 10
Valuation and Rates of Return

Valuation Concepts
    Concept of Yield to Maturity
    Changing the Yield to Maturity and the Impact on Bond Valuation
    Time to Maturity
    Determining Yield to Maturity from the Bond Price
    Semiannual Interest and Bond Prices

Valuation and Preferred Stock

Valuation of Common Stock
    No Growth in Dividends
    Determining the Required Rate of Return from the Market Price
    The Price-Earnings Ratio Concept and Valuation
    Variable Growth in Dividends

IRWIN © a Times Mirror Higher Education Group, Inc. company. 1997

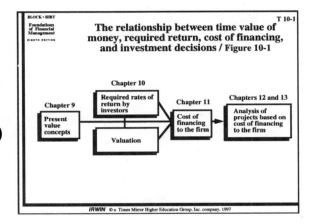

BLOCK • HIRT

Foundations
of Financial
Management

EIGHTH EDITION

T 10-1

The relationship between time value of money, required return, cost of financing, and investment decisions / Figure 10-1

Chapter 10

Chapter 9 — Present value concepts

Required rates of return by investors

Valuation

Chapter 11 — Cost of financing to the firm

Chapters 12 and 13 — Analysis of projects based on cost of financing to the firm

IRWIN © a Times Mirror Higher Education Group, Inc. company. 1997

BLOCK • HIRT

Foundations
of Financial
Management

EIGHTH EDITION

T 10-2

Bond price table / Table 10-1

(10 Percent Interest Payment, 20 Years to Maturity)

Yield to Maturity	Bond Price
2%	$2,308.10
4	1,825.00
6	1,459.00
7	1,317.40
8	1,196.80
9	1,090.90
10	1,000.00
11	920.30
12	850.90
13	789.50
14	735.30
16	643.90
20	513.00
25	407.40

IRWIN © a Times Mirror Higher Education Group, Inc. company. 1997

BLOCK · HIRT

Foundations
of Financial
Management

EIGHTH EDITION

T 10-3

Impact of time to maturity
on bond prices / Table 10-2

Time Period in Years (of 10 percent bond)	Bond Price with 8 Percent Yield to Maturity	Bond Price with 12 Percent Yield to Maturity
0	$1,000.00	$1,000.00
1	1,018.60	982.30
5	1,080.30	927.50
10	1,134.00	887.00
15	1,170.90	864.11
20	1,196.80	850.90
25	1,213.50	843.30
30	1,224.80	838.50

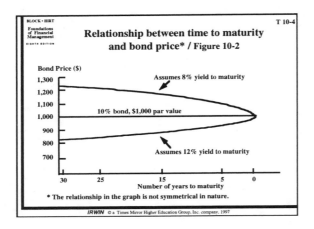

BLOCK · HIRT

Foundations
of Financial
Management

EIGHTH EDITION

T 10-4

Relationship between time to maturity
and bond price* / Figure 10-2

Bond Price ($)

Assumes 8% yield to maturity

10% bond, $1,000 par value

Assumes 12% yield to maturity

Number of years to maturity

* The relationship in the graph is not symmetrical in nature.

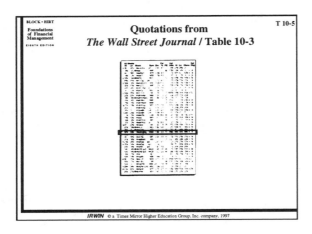

BLOCK · HIRT

Foundations
of Financial
Management

EIGHTH EDITION

T 10-5

Quotations from
The Wall Street Journal / Table 10-3

44

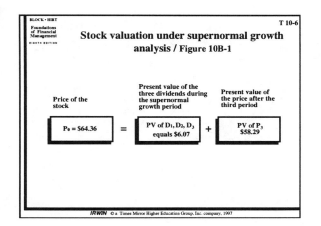

BLOCK • HIRT
Foundations
of Financial
Management
EIGHTH EDITION
T -CH11

Chapter 11
Cost of Capital

The Overall Concept

Cost of Debt

Cost of Preferred Stock

Cost of Common Equity

    Valuation Approach

    Cost of Retained Earnings

    Cost of New Common Stock

    Overview of Common Stock Costs

Optimal Capital Structure - Weighting Costs

Capital Acquisition and Investment Decision Making

The Marginal Cost of Capital

BLOCK • HIRT
Foundations
of Financial
Management
EIGHTH EDITION
T 11-1

Cost of capital –
Baker Corporation / Table 11-1

		(1) Cost (aftertax)	(2) Weights	(3) Weighted Cost
Debt	K_d	7.05%	30%	2.12%
Preferred stock	K_p	10.94	10	1.09
Common equity (retained earnings) . . .	K_e	12.00	60	7.20
Weighted average cost of capital	K_a			10.41%

BLOCK • HIRT
Foundations
of Financial
Management
EIGHTH EDITION
T 11-2

Cost of capital curve / Figure 11-1

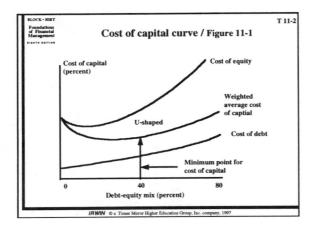

**Debt as a percentage of
total assets / Table 11-3**

Selected Companies, with Industry Designation	Percent
National Presto (electrical appliances)	17%
Mylan Labs (pharmaceuticals)	20
Diebold (automatic transmissions)	23
Liz Claiborne (women's clothing)	31
Sensormatic Electron (theft control)	37
Reebok International (footwear)	40
Motorola (electronics)	48
Gannett (newspaper and publishing)	54
Stanley Works (home tools)	56
Alcan Aluminum (aluminum products)	57
Fluor (engineering)	58
Playboy Enterprises (entertainment)	65
Union Carbide (petrochemicals)	69
PepsiCo (beverages and food)	75
Chrysler (automobiles)	80
Delta Airlines (air travel)	87

**Cost of capital
over time / Figure 11-2**

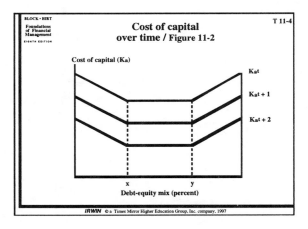

Cost of capital (K_a)

K_{at}

$K_{at} + 1$

$K_{at} + 2$

x   y

Debt-equity mix (percent)

**Investment projects available to
the Baker Corporation / Table 11-4**

Projects	Expected Returns	Cost ($ millions)
A	16.00%	$10
B	14.00	5
C	13.50	4
D	11.80	20
E	10.65	11
F	9.50	20
G	8.60	15
H	7.00	10
		$95 million

BLOCK · HIRT
Foundations
of Financial
Management
EIGHTH EDITION
T 11-6

Cost of capital and investment projects for the Baker Corporation / Figure 11-3

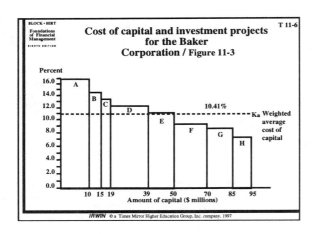

BLOCK · HIRT
Foundations
of Financial
Management
EIGHTH EDITION
T 11-7

Cost of capital for different amounts of financing / Table 11-5 (first part)

	First $39 Million				Next $11 Million		
		A/T Cost	Wts.	Weighted Cost		A/T Cost	Wts.	Weighted Cost
Debt	K_d	7.05%	.30	2.12%	Debt . . . K_d	7.05%	.30	2.12%
Preferred . .	K_p	10.94	.10	1.09	Preferred . K_p	10.94	.10	1.09
Common equity *. .	K_e	12.00	.60	7.20	Common equity † . . K_n	12.60	.60	7.56
			$K_a =$	10.41%			$K_{mc} =$	10.77%

*Retained earnings.   †New common stock.

BLOCK · HIRT
Foundations
of Financial
Management
EIGHTH EDITION
T 11-7

Cost of capital for increasing amounts of financing / Table 11-6 (final part)

Over $50 Million

		Cost (aftertax)	Weights	Weighted Cost
Debt (higher cost)	K_d	8.60%	.30	2.58%
Preferred stock	K_p	10.94	.10	1.09
Common equity (new common stock)	K_n	12.60	.60	7.56
			$K_{mc} =$	11.23%

Marginal cost of capital and Baker Corporation projects / Figure 11-4

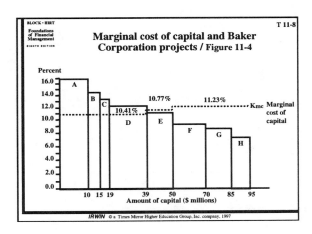

Cost of components in the capital structure / Table 11-7

1. Cost of debt K_d = Yield $(1 - T)$ = 7.05%

Yield = 10.84%
T = Corporate tax rate, 35%

2. Cost of preferred stock $K_p = \dfrac{D_p}{P_p - F}$ = 10.94%

D_p = Preferred dividend, \$10.50
P_p = Price of preferred stock, \$100
F = Flotation costs, \$4

3. Cost of common equity (retained earnings) $K_e = \dfrac{D_1}{P_0} + g$ = 12%

D_1 = First year common dividend, \$2
P_0 = Price of common stock, \$40
g = Growth rate, 7%

4. Cost of new common stock $K_n = \dfrac{D_1}{P_0 - F} + g$ = 12%

Same as above, with F = flotation costs, \$4

Review of formulas (first part)

1. K_d (cost of debt) = Y $(1 - T)$ (11-2)
Y is yield
T is corporate tax rate

2. K_p (cost of preferred stock) = $\dfrac{D_p}{P_p - F}$ (11-3)

D_p is the annual dividend on preferred stock
P_p is the price of preferred stock
F is flotation, or selling, cost

3. K_e (cost of common equity) = $\dfrac{D_1}{P_0} + g$ (11-4)

D_1 is dividend at the end of the first year (or period)   (11-5)
P_0 is the price of the stock today
g is growth rate in dividends

BLOCK · HIRT
Foundations
of Financial
Management
EIGHTH EDITION

T 11-10

Review of formulas (second part)

4. K_j (required return on common stock) $= R_f + \beta (K_m - R_f)$ (11-5)

   R_f is risk-free rate of return
   β is beta coefficient
   K_m is return in the market as measured by the appropriate
   index

5. K_e (cost of common equity in
   the form of retained earnings) $= \dfrac{D_1}{P_0} + g$ (11-6)

   D_1 is the dividend at the end of the first year (or period)
   P_0 is the price of the stock today
   g is growth rate in dividends

6. K_n (cost of new common stock) $= \dfrac{D_1}{P_0 - F} + g$ (11-7)

   Same as above, with:
   F as flotation, or selling, cost

IRWIN © a Times Mirror Higher Education Group, Inc. company, 1997

BLOCK · HIRT
Foundations
of Financial
Management
EIGHTH EDITION

T 11-10

Review of formulas (final part)

7. X (size of capital
   structure that retained $= \dfrac{\text{Retained earnings}}{\text{\% of retained earnings in}}$ (11-8)
   earnings will support)   the capital structure

8. Z (size of capital
   structure that lower-cost $= \dfrac{\text{Amount of lower-cost debt}}{\text{\% of debt in the}}$
   debt will support)   capital structure   (11-9)

IRWIN © a Times Mirror Higher Education Group, Inc. company, 1997

BLOCK · HIRT
Foundations
of Financial
Management
EIGHTH EDITION

T 11-11

Performance of PAI and the market /
Table 11A-1

Year	Rate of Return on Stock	
	PAI	Market
1	12.0%	10.0%
2	16.0	18.0
3	20.0	16.0
4	16.0	10.0
5	6.0	8.0
Mean return	14.0%	12.4%
Standard deviation	4.73%	3.87%

IRWIN © a Times Mirror Higher Education Group, Inc. company, 1997

Linear regression of returns between PAI and the market /
Figure 11A-1 (first part)

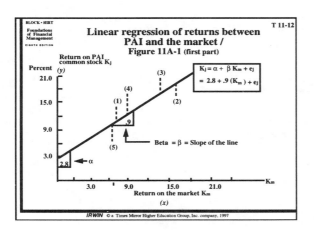

$$K_J = \alpha + \beta K_m + e_J$$
$$= 2.8 + .9 (K_m) + e_J$$

Beta $= \beta$ = Slope of the line

Linear regression of returns between PAI and the market /
Figure 11A-1 (final part)

Year	K_J	K_m	$\Sigma K_J K_m$ 936	$\Sigma K_J \Sigma K_m$ 4,340	$\Sigma K_m{}^2$ 844	$(\Sigma K_m)^2$ 3,844
1.....	12%	10%				
2.....	16%	18%				
3.....	20%	16%				
4.....	16%	10%				
5.....	6%	8%				
	70%	62%				

$$\beta = \frac{n \Sigma K_J K_m - \Sigma K_J K_m}{n \Sigma K_m{}^2 - (\Sigma K_m)^2} = \frac{5(936) - 4,340}{5(844) - 3,844} = 0.9$$

$$\alpha = \frac{\Sigma K_J - \beta \Sigma K_m}{n} = \frac{70 - 0.9(62)}{5} = 2.8$$

The security market line (SML) / Figure 11A-2

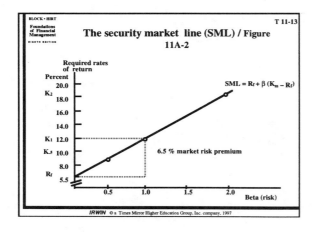

$$SML = R_f + \beta (K_m - R_f)$$

6.5 % market risk premium

51

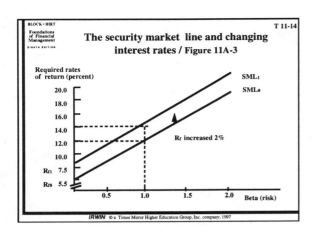

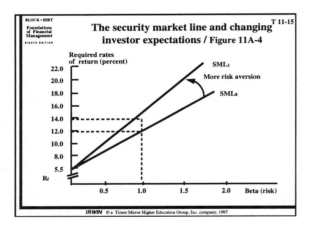

52

BLOCK • HIRT
Foundations
of Financial
Management
EIGHTH EDITION

T-CH12

Chapter 12
The Capital Budgeting Decision

Administrative Considerations

Accounting Flows versus Cash Flows

Methods of Ranking Investment Proposals

Selection Strategy

Capital Rationing

Net Present Value Profile

Combining Cash Flow Analysis and Selection Strategy

Actual Investment Decision

Elective Expensing

BLOCK • HIRT
Foundations
of Financial
Management
EIGHTH EDITION

T 12-1

Capital budgeting procedures /
Figure 12-1

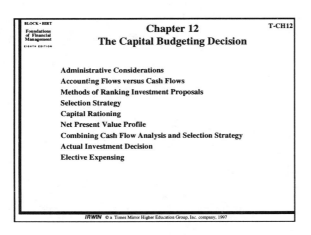

BLOCK • HIRT
Foundations
of Financial
Management
EIGHTH EDITION

T 12-2

Cash flow for Alston Corporation /
Table 12-1 (first part)

Earnings before depreciation and taxes (cash inflow) . . .	$20,000
Depreciation (noncash expense)	5,000
Earnings before taxes	5,000
Taxes (cash outflow)	5,250
Earnings after taxes	9,750
Depreciation	+ 5,000
Cash flow	$14,750
Cash inflow (EBDT)	$20,000
Cash outflow (taxes)	- 5,250
Cash flow	$14,750

BLOCK · HIRT
Foundations
of Financial
Management
EIGHTH EDITION

Revised cash flow for Alston Corporation /
Table 12-2 (final part)

Earnings before depreciation and taxes	$20,000
Depreciation	20,000
Earnings before taxes	0
Taxes	0
Earnings after taxes	0
Depreciation	+ 20,000
Cash flow	$20,000

IRWIN © a Times Mirror Higher Education Group, Inc. company, 1997

BLOCK · HIRT
Foundations
of Financial
Management
EIGHTH EDITION

Investment alternatives /
Table 12-3 (first part)

Year	Cash Inflows (of $10,000 investment)	
	Investment A	Investment B
1 . . .	$5,000	$1,500
2 . . .	5,000	2,000
3 . . .	2,000	2,500
4 . . .		5,000
5 . . .		5,000

IRWIN © a Times Mirror Higher Education Group, Inc. company, 1997

BLOCK · HIRT
Foundations
of Financial
Management
EIGHTH EDITION

Capital budgeting results /
Table 12-4 (final part)

	Investment A	Investment B	Selection
Payback method	2 years	3.8 years	Quicker payout: Investment A
Internal rate of return . .	11.17%	14.33%	Higher yield: Investment B
Net present value	$177	$1,414	Higher net present value: Investment B

IRWIN © a Times Mirror Higher Education Group, Inc. company, 1997

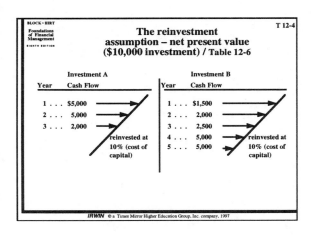

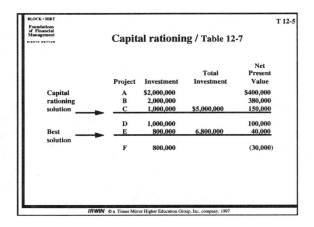

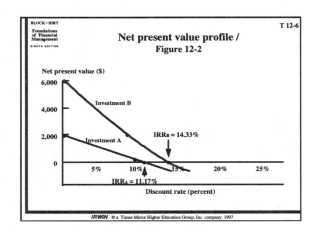

55

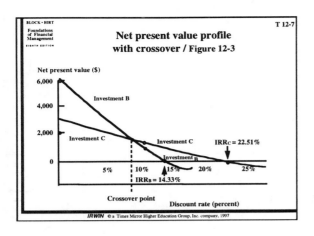

Net present value profile with crossover / Figure 12-3

Categories of depreciation write-off /
Table 12-8 (first part)

Class

3-year MACRS	All property with ADR midpoints of four years or less. Autos and light trucks are excluded from this category.
5-year MACRS	Property with ADR midpoints of more than 4, but less than 10 years. Key assets in this category include automobiles, light trucks, and technological equipment such as computers and research-related properties.
7-year MACRS	Property with ADR midpoints of 10 years or more, but less than 16 years. Most types of manufacturing equipment would fall into this category, as would office furniture and fixtures.
10-year MACRS	Property with ADR midpoints of 16 years or more, but less than 20 years. Petroleum refining products, railroad tank cars, and manufactured homes fall into this group.

Categories of depreciation write-off /
Table 12-8 (final part)

Class

15-year MACRS	Property with ADR midpoints of 20 years or more, but less than 25 years. Land improvement, pipeline distribution, telephone distribution, and sewage treatment plants all belong in this category.
20-year MACRS	Property with ADR midpoints 25 years or more (with the exception of real estate, which is treated separately). Key investments in this category include electric and gas utility property and sewer pipes.
27.5-year MACRS	Residential rental property if 80% or more of the gross rental income is from nontransient dwelling units (e.g., an apartment building); low-income housing.
31.5-year MACRS	Nonresidential real property that has no ADR class life or whose class life is 27.5 years or more.
39-year MACRS	Nonresidential real property placed in service after May 12, 1993

BLOCK · HIRT

Foundations
of Financial
Management
EIGHTH EDITION

T 12-9

Depreciation percentages (expressed in decimals) / Table 12-9

Depreciation Year	3-Year MACRS	5-Year MACRS	7-Year MACRS	10-Year MACRS	15-Year MACRS	20-Year MACRS
1 . . .	.333	.200	.143	.100	.050	.038
2 . . .	.445	.320	.245	.180	.095	.072
3 . . .	.148	.192	.175	.144	.086	.067
4 . . .	.074	.115	.125	.115	.077	.062
5 . . .		.115	.089	.092	.069	.057
6 . . .		.058	.089	.074	.062	.053
7 . . .			.089	.066	.059	.045
8 . . .			.045	.066	.059	.045
9 . . .				.065	.059	.045
10 . . .				.065	.059	.045
11 . . .				.033	.059	.045
12 . . .					.059	.045
13 . . .					.059	.045
14 . . .					.059	.045
15 . . .					.059	.045
16 . . .					.030	.045
17 . . .						.045
18 . . .						.045
19 . . .						.045
20 . . .						.045
21 . . .						.017
	1.000	1.000	1.000	1.000	1.000	1.000

BLOCK · HIRT

Foundations
of Financial
Management
EIGHTH EDITION

T 12-10

Depreciation schedule / Table 12-10

(1) Year	(2) Depreciation Base	(3) Percentage Depreciation (Table 12-9)	(4) Annual Depreciation
1	$50,000	.200	$10,000
2	50,000	.320	16,000
3	50,000	.192	9,600
4	50,000	.115	5,750
5	50,000	.115	5,750
6	50,000	.058	2,900
		Total Depreciation	$50,000

BLOCK · HIRT

Foundations
of Financial
Management
EIGHTH EDITION

T 12-11

Cash flow related to the purchase of machinery / Table 12-11

	Year 1	Year 2	Year 3	Year 4	Year 5	Year 6
Earnings before depreciation and taxes (EBDT)	$18,500	$18,500	$18,500	$12,000	$12,000	$12,000
Depreciation (from Table 12-10)	10,000	16,000	9,600	5,750	5,750	2,900
Earnings before taxes	8,500	2,500	8,900	6,250	6,250	9,100
Taxes (35%)	2,975	875	3,115	2,188	2,188	3,185
Earnings after taxes	5,525	1,625	5,785	4,062	4,062	5,915
+ Depreciation	10,000	16,000	9,600	5,750	5,750	2,900
Cash flow	$15,525	$17,625	$15,385	$9,812	$9,812	$8,815

BLOCK · HIRT
Foundations
of Financial
Management
EIGHTH EDITION

T 12-12

Net present value
analysis / Table 12-12

Year	Cash Flow (inflows)	Present Value Factor (10%)	Present Value
1	$15,525	.909	$14,112
2	17,625	.826	14,558
3	15,385	.751	11,554
4	9,812	.683	6,702
5	9,812	.621	6,093
6	8,815	.564	4,972
			$57,991

Present value of inflows	$57,991
Present value of outflows (cost)	50,000
Net present value	$ 7,991

BLOCK · HIRT
Foundations
of Financial
Management
EIGHTH EDITION

T 12-13

Analysis of incremental depreciation
benefits / Table 12-15

(1) Year	(2) Depreciation on New Computer	(3) Depreciation on Old Computer	(4) Incremental Depreciation	(5) Tax Rate	(6) Tax Shield Benefits
1 . . .	$36,000	$23,040	$12,960	.35	$ 4,536
2 . . .	57,600	13,800	43,800	.35	15,330
3 . . .	34,560	13,800	20,760	.35	7,266
4 . . .	20,700	6,960	13,740	.35	4,809
5 . . .	20,700		20,700	.35	7,245
6 . . .	10,440		10,440	.35	3,645

BLOCK · HIRT
Foundations
of Financial
Management
EIGHTH EDITION

T 12-14

Analysis of incremental cost savings
benefits / Table 12-16

(1) Year	(2) Cost Savings	(3) 1 — Tax Rate	(4) Aftertax Savings
1	$42,000	.65	$27,300
2	42,000	.65	27,300
3	42,000	.65	27,300
4	42,000	.65	27,300
5	42,000	.65	27,300
6	42,000	.65	27,300

58

BLOCK • HIRT

Foundations
of Financial
Management

EIGHTH EDITION

Present value of the total incremental benefits / Table 12-17

(1) Year	(2) Tax Shield Benefits from Depreciation (from Table 12-15)	(3) Aftertax Cost Savings (from Table 12-16)	(4) Total Annual Benefits	(5) Present Value Factor (10%)	(6) Present Value
1 . . .	$ 4,536	$27,300	$31,836	.909	$28,939
2 . . .	15,330	27,300	42,630	.826	35,212
3 . . .	7,266	27,300	34,566	.751	25,959
4 . . .	4,809	27,300	32,109	.683	21,930
5 . . .	7,245	27,300	34,545	.621	21,452
6 . . .	3,645	27,300	30,945	.564	17,453
		Present value of incremental benefits			$150,945

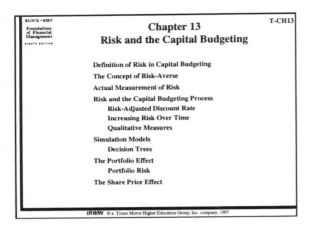

IRWIN © a Times Mirror Higher Education Group, Inc. company, 1997

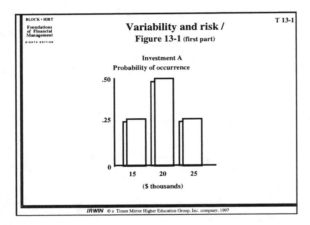

Variability and risk /
Figure 13-1 (first part)

T 13-1

Investment A
Probability of occurrence

IRWIN © a Times Mirror Higher Education Group, Inc. company, 1997

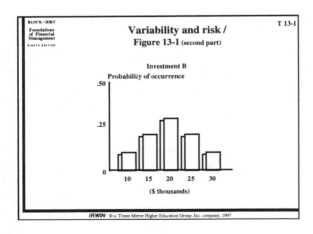

Variability and risk /
Figure 13-1 (second part)

T 13-1

Investment B
Probability of occurrence

IRWIN © a Times Mirror Higher Education Group, Inc. company, 1997

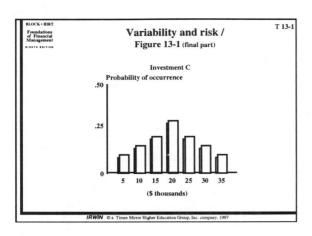

Variability and risk /
Figure 13-1 (final part)

T 13-1

Investment C

Probability of occurrence

.50

.25

0

5   10   15   20   25   30   35

($ thousands)

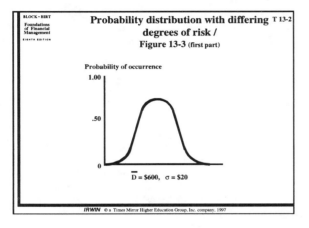

Probability distribution with differing degrees of risk /
Figure 13-3 (first part)

T 13-2

Probability of occurrence

1.00

.50

0

$\overline{D} = \$600, \quad \sigma = \$20$

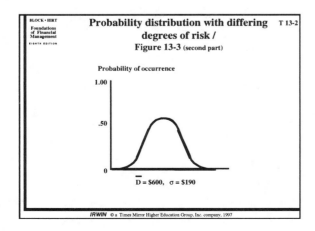

Probability distribution with differing degrees of risk /
Figure 13-3 (second part)

T 13-2

Probability of occurrence

1.00

.50

0

$\overline{D} = \$600, \quad \sigma = \$190$

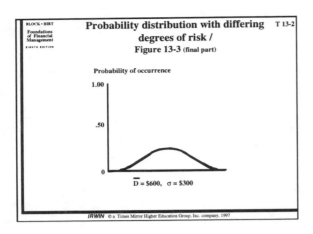

BLOCK · HIRT
Foundations
of Financial
Management
EIGHTH EDITION

Probability distribution with differing degrees of risk /
Figure 13-3 (final part)

Probability of occurrence

1.00

.50

0

$\overline{D} = \$600, \quad \sigma = \$300$

IRWIN © a Times Mirror Higher Education Group, Inc. company, 1997

BLOCK · HIRT
Foundations
of Financial
Management
EIGHTH EDITION

Betas for a five-year period
(1990–1995) / Table 13-2

Company Name	Beta
Central Louisiana Electric	.60
Tootsie Roll Industries	.70
Jefferson-Pilot Group	.80
Phillips Petroleum	.90
Rockwell International	.95
Standard & Poor's 500 Stock Index	1.00
General Motors	1.10
Tommy Hilfiger	1.25
Deere & Co.	1.35
Home Depot	1.55
Merrill Lynch & Co.	1.90

IRWIN © a Times Mirror Higher Education Group, Inc. company, 1997

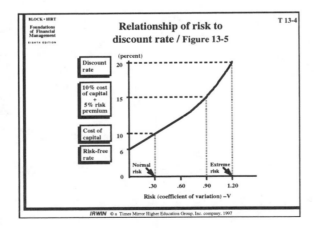

BLOCK · HIRT
Foundations
of Financial
Management
EIGHTH EDITION

Relationship of risk to
discount rate / Figure 13-5

(percent)

Discount rate

10% cost of capital + 5% risk premium

Cost of capital

Risk-free rate

Normal risk

Extreme risk

20

15

10

6

0

.30   .60   .90   1.20

Risk (coefficient of variation) –V

IRWIN © a Times Mirror Higher Education Group, Inc. company, 1997

Risk over time / Figure 13-6

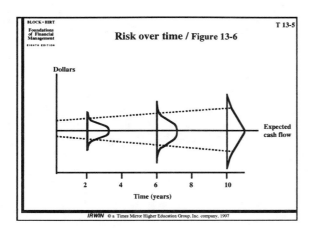

Capital budgeting analysis /
Table 13-4

Year	Investment A (10% discount rate)	Year	Investment B (10% discount rate)
1	$5,000 × 0.909 = $4,545	1	$1,500 × 0.909 = $1,364
2	5,000 × 0.826 = 4,130	2	2,000 × 0.826 = 1,652
3	2,000 × 0.751 = 1,502	3	2,500 × 0.751 = 1,878
	$10,177	4	5,000 × 0.683 = 3,415
		5	5,000 × 0.621 = 3,105
			$11,414

Present value of inflows	$ 10,177	Present value of inflows	$11,414
Investment	−10,000	Investment	−10,000
Net present value	$ 177	Net present value	$ 1,414

Capital budgeting decision
adjusted for risk / Table 13-5

Year	Investment A (10% discount rate)	Year	Investment B (20% discount rate)
1	$5,000 × 0.909 = $4,545	1	$1,500 × 0.833 = $1,250
2	5,000 × 0.826 = 4,130	2	2,000 × 0.694 = 1,388
3	2,000 × 0.751 = 1,502	3	2,500 × 0.579 = 1,448
	$10,177	4	5,000 × 0.482 = 2,410
		5	5,000 × 0.402 = 2,010
			$ 8,506

Present value of inflows	$10,177	Present value of inflows	$ 8,506
Investment	−10,000	Investment	−10,000
Net present value	$ 177	Net present value	$ (1,494)

63

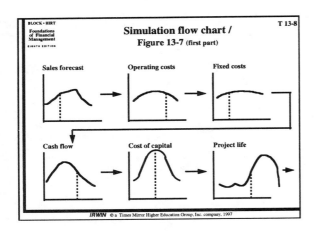

BLOCK · HIRT

T 13-8

Foundations
of Financial
Management

EIGHTH EDITION

Simulation flow chart /
Figure 13-7 (first part)

Sales forecast → Operating costs → Fixed costs

Cash flow → Cost of capital → Project life →

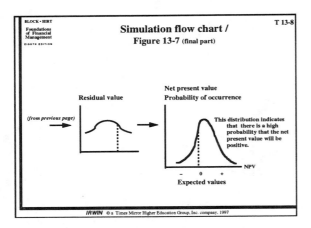

BLOCK · HIRT

T 13-8

Foundations
of Financial
Management

EIGHTH EDITION

Simulation flow chart /
Figure 13-7 (final part)

Net present value
Probability of occurrence

Residual value

(from previous page) →

This distribution indicates
that there is a high
probability that the net
present value will be
positive.

NPV

– 0 +

Expected values

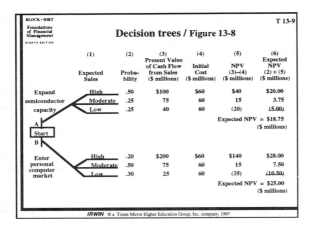

BLOCK · HIRT

T 13-9

Foundations
of Financial
Management

EIGHTH EDITION

Decision trees / Figure 13-8

	(1) Expected Sales	(2) Proba- bility	(3) Present Value of Cash Flow from Sales ($ millions)	(4) Initial Cost ($ millions)	(5) NPV (3)–(4) ($ millions)	(6) Expected NPV (2) × (5) ($ millions)
Expand semiconductor capacity	High	.50	$100	$60	$40	$20.00
	Moderate	.25	75	60	15	3.75
	Low	.25	40	60	(20)	(5.00)
					Expected NPV =	$18.75 ($ millions)
A						
Start						
B						
Enter personal computer market	High	.20	$200	$60	$140	$28.00
	Moderate	.50	75	60	15	7.50
	Low	.30	25	60	(35)	(10.50)
					Expected NPV =	$25.00 ($ millions)

64

BLOCK · HIRT
Foundations
of Financial
Management
EIGHTH EDITION
T 13-10

Rates of return for Conglomerate, Inc. and two merger candidates / Table 13-7

Year	(1) Conglomerate, Inc.	(2) Positive Correlation, Inc. +1.0	(3) Negative Correlation, Inc. −.9	(1) + (2) Conglomerate, Inc. + Positive Correlation, Inc.	(1) + (3) Conglomerate, Inc. + Negative Correlation, Inc.
1	14%	16%	10%	15%	12%
2	10	12	16	11	13
3	8	10	18	9	13
4	12	14	14	13	13
5	16	18	12	17	14
Mean return	12%	14%	14%	13%	13%
Standard deviation of returns (σ)	2.82%	2.82%	2.82%	2.82%	.63%
Correlation coefficients with Conglomerate, Inc.				+1.0	−.9

BLOCK · HIRT
Foundations
of Financial
Management
EIGHTH EDITION
T 13-11

Risk-return trade-offs / Figure 13-11

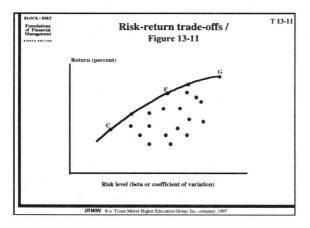

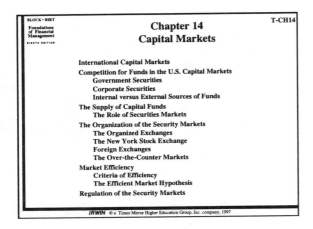

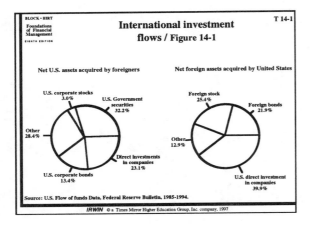

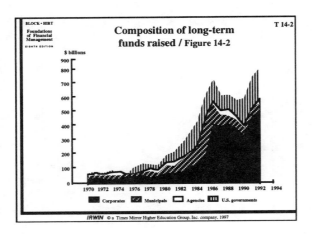

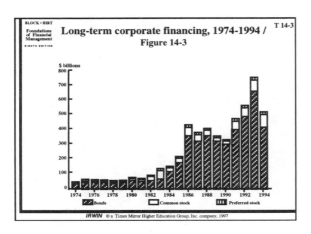

Long-term corporate financing, 1974-1994 / Figure 14-3

T 14-3

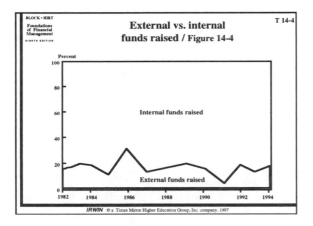

External vs. internal funds raised / Figure 14-4

T 14-4

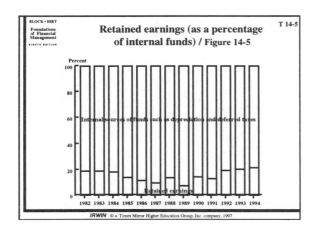

Retained earnings (as a percentage of internal funds) / Figure 14-5

T 14-5

Flow of funds through the eonomy / Figure 14-6

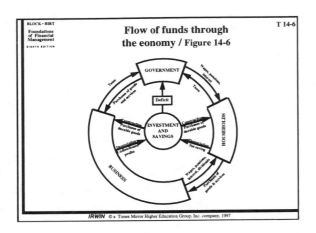

Global stock markets / Table 14-1

Australia	Mexico
Austria	Netherlands
Belgium	Norway
Canada	Singapore/Malaysia
Denmark	Spain
France	Sweden
Germany	Switzerland
Hong Kong	United Kingdom
Italy	United States
Japan	

Chapter 15 Investment Banking: Public and Private Placement

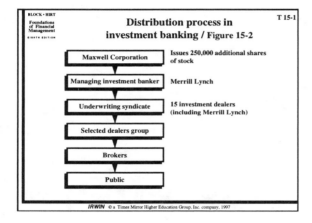

Distribution process in investment banking / Figure 15-2

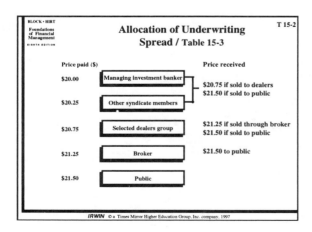

Allocation of Underwriting Spread / Table 15-3

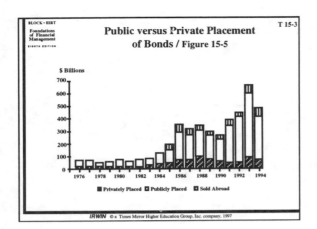

BLOCK · HIRT
Foundations
of Financial
Management
EIGHTH EDITION

**Public versus Private Placement
of Bonds / Figure 15-5**

$ Billions

700
600
500
400
300
200
100
0

1976   1978   1980   1982   1984   1986   1988   1990   1992   1994

■ Privately Placed   ☐ Publicly Placed   ☒ Sold Abroad

IRWIN   © a Times Mirror Higher Education Group, Inc. company, 1997

70

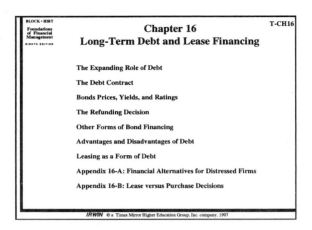

Chapter 16
Long-Term Debt and Lease Financing

T-CH16

BLOCK · HIRT
Foundations of Financial Management
EIGHTH EDITION

The Expanding Role of Debt

The Debt Contract

Bonds Prices, Yields, and Ratings

The Refunding Decision

Other Forms of Bond Financing

Advantages and Disadvantages of Debt

Leasing as a Form of Debt

Appendix 16-A: Financial Alternatives for Distressed Firms

Appendix 16-B: Lease versus Purchase Decisions

IRWIN © a Times Mirror Higher Education Group, Inc. company. 1997

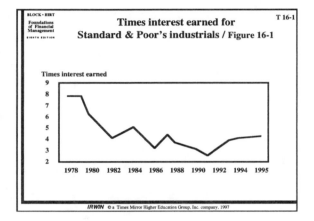

Times interest earned for
Standard & Poor's industrials / Figure 16-1

T 16-1

BLOCK · HIRT
Foundations of Financial Management
EIGHTH EDITION

Times interest earned

IRWIN © a Times Mirror Higher Education Group, Inc. company. 1997

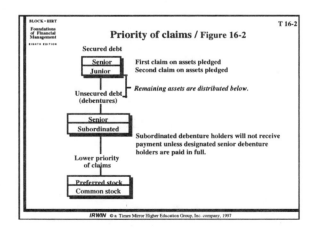

Priority of claims / Figure 16-2

T 16-2

BLOCK · HIRT
Foundations of Financial Management
EIGHTH EDITION

Secured debt

Senior — First claim on assets pledged
Junior — Second claim on assets pledged

Remaining assets are distributed below.

Unsecured debt (debentures)

Senior
Subordinated

Subordinated debenture holders will not receive payment unless designated senior debenture holders are paid in full.

Lower priority of claims

Preferred stock
Common stock

IRWIN © a Times Mirror Higher Education Group, Inc. company. 1997

Bond Price Table / Table 16-3

Interest rates and bond prices (the bond pays 12 percent interest)

Years to Maturity	Rate in the Market (percent) — Yield to Maturity*				
	8%	10%	12%	14%	16%
1	$1,038.16	$1,018.54	$1,000	$981.48	$963.98
15	1,345.52	1,153.32	1,000	875.54	774.48
25	1,429.92	1,182.36	1,000	862.06	754.98

*The prices in the table are based on semi annual interest, but you enter it with annual values.

Restatement of Facts

	Old Issue	New Issue
Size	$10,000,000	$10,000,000
Interest rate	11.75%	9.5%
Total life	25 years	20 years
Remaining life	20 years	20 years
Call premium	10%	--
Underwriting costs . .	$125,000	$200,000

Tax bracket 35%
Discount rate 6%

Step C—Net Present Value

We now compare our outflows and our inflows from the prior pages.

Outflows			Inflows	
1. Net cost of call premium. . .	$650,000		3. Cost savings in lower interest rates . . .	$1,677,488
2. Net cost of under-writing expense on new issue . . .	159,855		4. Net gain from under-writing cost on old issue	14,928
	$809,855			$1,692,416

Present value of inflows . . . $ 1,692,416
Present value of outflows . . . 809,855

Net present value . . . . . $ 882,561

BLOCK · HIRT

Foundations
of Financial
Management

EIGHTH EDITION

T 16-6

Zero-Coupon and Floating
Rate Bonds / Table 16-5

	Rating	Coupon	Maturity	Price	Yield to Maturity
Zero-coupon bonds:					
Hospital Corp. of America	A3	0.00%	2000	$713.75	6.83%
Clark USA, Inc.	B1	0.00%	2000	$571.25	12.24%
Floating rate bonds:					
CIT Group Holdings, Inc.	Not Rated	6.75%	2004	$995.00	6.82%

Source: *Moody's Bond Record,* June 1995.

BLOCK · HIRT

Foundations
of Financial
Management

EIGHTH EDITION

T 16-7

Examples of Eurobonds / Table 16-6

	Rating	Coupon	Maturity	Amount Outstanding ($ millions)	Currency Denomination*
Merrill Lynch & Co., Inc. †	A1	0.00%	2000	100.0	DM
Nippon Telephone & Telegraph	Aaa	10.25%	2001	200.0	U.S.$
Petro-Canada	Baa1	9.25%	2021	300.0	U.S.$
Procter & Gamble Co.	Aa2	10.88%	2001	200.0	C$
Sony Corporation	Aa3	1.40%	2005	300.0	Yen
Telecom Corporation	Aa1	7.50%	2003	100.0	N Z$

*DM is Deutsche mark, N Z $ is New Zealand dollar, and C$ is Canadian dollar.
†This is a zero-coupon rate bond.
Source: *Moody's Bond Record,* July 1995.

BLOCK • HIRT

Foundations
of Financial
Management

EIGHTH EDITION

T-CH17

Chapter 17
Common and Preferred
Stock Financing

Common Stockholder's Claim to Income

The Voting Right
    Cumulative Voting

The Right to Purchase New Shares
    The Use of Rights in Financing
    Effects of Rights on Stockholder's Position
    Desirable Features of Rights Offerings
    Poison Pill

American Depository Receipts

Preferred Stock Financing
    Justification for Preferred Stock

Provisions Associated with Preferred Stock

Comparing Feature of Common and Preferred Stock and Debt

BLOCK • HIRT

Foundations
of Financial
Management

EIGHTH EDITION

T-17-1

Institutional ownership of
U.S. companies / Table 17-1 (first part)

	Number of Institutions	Percent Owned	Ownership in $ Millions
General Electric	880	50.4	$46,581
Coca-Cola Co.	755	52.2	37,491
Exxon	806	39.8	32,937
Phillip Morris Cos Inc.	752	55.7	31,055
AT&T	836	34.3	27,863
Intel Corp.	740	71.8	25,284
Merck & Co.	815	47.3	25,035
Int'l Business Machines Corp.	737	48.1	23,240
Johnson & Johnson	793	58.9	22,532
Procter & Gamble Co.	708	46.8	21,328
Motorola Inc.	759	63.6	20,390
Mobil Corp.	736	51.8	18,997
Amoco Corp.	701	59.1	18,700
Du Pont Co.	650	44.2	18,239

BLOCK • HIRT

Foundations
of Financial
Management

EIGHTH EDITION

T-17-1

Institutional ownership of
U.S. companies / Table 17-1 (final part)

	Number of Institutions	Percent Owned	Ownership in $ Millions
General Motors Corp.	582	54.6	$18,134
Hewlett-Packard Co.	668	57.7	17,706
PepsiCo Inc.	725	56.5	17,538
American International Group Inc.	647	52.1	17,157
Wal-Mart Stores	626	28.2	16,611
Pfizer Inc.	687	60.5	16,319
Microsoft Corp.	615	37.3	15,452
Bristol-Myers Squibb Co.	739	47.3	15,199
GTE Corp.	686	39.1	12,600
Ford Motor Co.	567	43.1	11,874
Bell South Corp.	566	28.8	8,491

74

BLOCK · HIRT
Foundations
of Financial
Management
EIGHTH EDITION
T-17-2

Before-tax yields on corporate bonds and high-grade preferred stock / Table 17-2

Year	As Bond Yields	Moody's High-Grade Preferred Stock Yields	Yield Spread Bonds/Preferred Stock
1977	8.24	7.12	1.12
1978	8.92	7.76	1.16
1979	9.94	8.54	1.40
1980	12.50	10.11	2.39
1981	14.75	11.64	3.11
1982	14.41	11.68	2.73
1983	12.42	10.05	2.37
1984	13.31	10.21	3.10
1985	11.82	9.41	2.41
1986	9.47	8.13	1.34
1987	9.68	7.94	1.74
1988	9.94	8.17	1.77
1989	9.46	7.82	1.64
1990	9.56	8.28	1.28
1991	9.05	7.87	1.18
1992	8.46	7.05	1.41
1993	7.40	6.32	1.08
1994	8.15	6.96	1.19
1995e	8.34	7.18	1.16

BLOCK · HIRT
Foundations
of Financial
Management
EIGHTH EDITION
T-17-3

Features of alternative security issues / Table 17-3 (first part)

	Common Stock	Preferred Stock	Bonds
1. Ownership and control of the firm	Belongs to common stockholders through voting right and residual claim to income	Limited rights when dividends are missed	Limited rights under default in interest payments
2. Obligation to provide return	None	Must receive payment before common stockholder	Contractual obligation
3. Claim to assets in bankruptcy	Lowest claim of any security holder	Bondholders and creditors must be satisfied first	Highest claim
4. Cost of distribution	Highest	Moderate	Lowest

BLOCK · HIRT
Foundations
of Financial
Management
EIGHTH EDITION
T-17-3

Features of alternative security issues / Table 17-3 (final part)

	Common Stock	Preferred Stock	Bonds
5. Risk-return trade-off	Highest risk, highest return (at least in theory)	Moderate risk, moderate return	Lowest risk, moderate return
6. Tax status of payment by corporation	Not deductible	Not deductible	Tax deductible Cost = Interest payment × (1 – Tax rate)
7. Tax status of payment to recipient	70 percent of dividend to another corporation is tax exempt	Same as common stock	Municipal bond interest is tax exempt

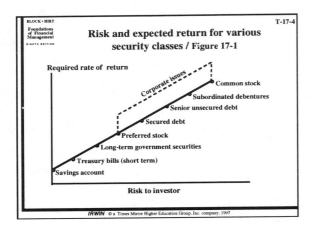

Risk and expected return for various security classes / Figure 17-1

Required rate of return

Corporate issues

Common stock

Subordinated debentures

Senior unsecured debt

Secured debt

Preferred stock

Long-term government securities

Treasury bills (short term)

Savings account

Risk to investor

Review of formulas (first part)

1. $\text{Shares required} = \dfrac{\text{Number of directors desired} \times \text{Total number of shares outstanding}}{\text{Total number of directors to be elected} + 1} + 1$ (17-1)

2. Number of directors that can be elected   (17-2)

$$= \dfrac{(\text{Shares owned} - 1) \times (\text{Total number of directors to be elected} + 1)}{(\text{Total number of shares outstanding})}$$

Review of formulas (final part)

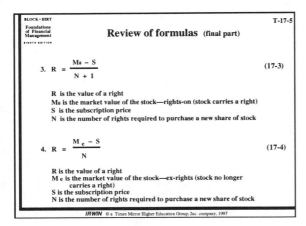

3. $R = \dfrac{M_0 - S}{N + 1}$ (17-3)

R is the value of a right
M_0 is the market value of the stock—rights-on (stock carries a right)
S is the subscription price
N is the number of rights required to purchase a new share of stock

4. $R = \dfrac{M_e - S}{N}$ (17-4)

R is the value of a right
M_e is the market value of the stock—ex-rights (stock no longer carries a right)
S is the subscription price
N is the number of rights required to purchase a new share of stock

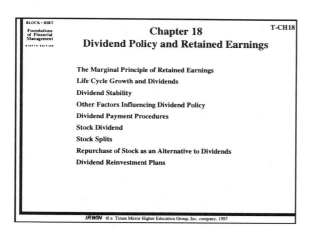

Chapter 18
Dividend Policy and Retained Earnings

The Marginal Principle of Retained Earnings

Life Cycle Growth and Dividends

Dividend Stability

Other Factors Influencing Dividend Policy

Dividend Payment Procedures

Stock Dividend

Stock Splits

Repurchase of Stock as an Alternative to Dividends

Dividend Reinvestment Plans

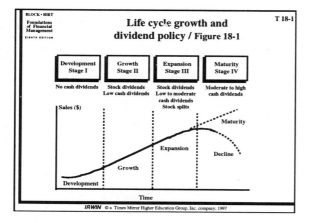

Life cycle growth and
dividend policy / Figure 18-1

T 18-1

Corporate dividend policy / Table 18-1

T 18-2

	Historical Growth in EPS (1991-95)	Estimated Growth in EPS* (1998-2000)	Dividend Payout as Percent of Aftertax Earnings (1995)
Category 1—Rapid Growth			
Amgen, Inc.	45%	25%	0%
Dell Computer	50%	20%	0%
Microsoft Corp.	35%	30%	0%
Tommy Hilfiger	43%	22%	0%
Category 2—Slow Growth			
Central Hudson	3%	3%	77%
Detroit Edison	3%	2%	72%
Exxon	4%	5%	60%
Northeast Utilities	1%	7%	82%

* Estimated growth from various issues of *Value Line Investment Survey.*

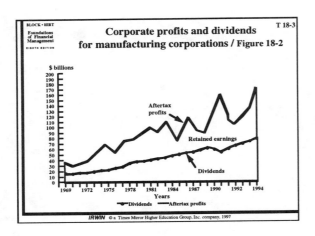

BLOCK · HIRT

Foundations
of Financial
Management
EIGHTH EDITION

T 18-3

Corporate profits and dividends
for manufacturing corporations / Figure 18-2

$ billions

Aftertax
profits

Retained earnings

Dividends

Years

—▼—Dividends   ——Aftertax profits

BLOCK · HIRT

Foundations
of Financial
Management
EIGHTH EDITION

T 18-4

XYZ Corporation's financial
position before stock dividend / Table 18-3

Capital
accounts

{

Common stock (1,000,000 shares at $10 par) $10,000,000
Capital in excess of par   5,000,000
Retained earnings   15,000,000

Net worth. $30,000,000

BLOCK · HIRT

Foundations
of Financial
Management
EIGHTH EDITION

T 18-4

XYZ Corporation's financial
position after stock dividend / Table 18-4

Capital
accounts

{

Common stock (1,100,000 shares at $10 par) . $11,000,000
Capital in excess of par   5,500,000
Retained earnings   13,500,000

Net worth. $30,000,000

BLOCK • HIRT
Foundations
of Financial
Management
EIGHTH EDITION
T 18-5

XYZ Corporation before and after stock split / Table 18-5

	Before	
Common stock (1 million shares at $10 par)		$10,000,000
Capital in excess of par		5,000,000
Retained earnings		15,000,000
		$30,000,000
	After	
Common stock (2 million shares at $5 par)		$10,000,000
Capital in excess of par		5,000,000
Retained earnings		15,000,000
		$30,000,000

BLOCK • HIRT
Foundations
of Financial
Management
EIGHTH EDITION
T 18-6

Stock repurchases: Biggest announced stock buybacks of 1987 / Table 18-7 (first part)

Company	Common Shares (in millions)	Value
General Motors	64.0	$4.72 billion
Santa Fe Southern Pacific	60.0	3.38 billion
Ford	27.9	2.00 billion
Coca-Cola	40.0	1.80 billion
Henley Group	64.5	1.76 billion
Gencorp	12.5	1.63 billion
IBM	12.9	1.57 billion
American Express	40.0	1.35 billion
Allied-Signal	25.0	1.11 billion
Owens-Illinois	20.0	1.11 billion
J.C. Penney	20.0	1.04 billion

Note: Figures represent announcements, not actual purchases, and may include more than one announcement. Values are actual dollar amounts when available or estimates based on closing prices before announcements. Reprinted by permission of *The Wall Street Journal*, Dow Jones and Company, Inc., January 4, 1987, p.8B. All rights reserved. Source: Merrill Lynch & Co.

BLOCK • HIRT
Foundations
of Financial
Management
EIGHTH EDITION
T 18-6

Stock repurchases: Biggest announced stock buybacks of 1987 / Table 18-7 (second part)

Company	Common Shares (in millions)	Value
Hercules	15.0	1.02 billion
IC Industries	30.8	1.00 billion
Merck	5.4	1.00 billion
Philip Morris	10.0	933.5 million
Bristol-Myers	25.0	925.0 million
NCR	14.0	825.3 million
Procter & Gamble	10.0	810.0 million
Salomon	21.3	808.7 million
Hewlett-Packard	15.3	750.0 million
Nynex	10.0	736.3 million
Chrysler	27.0	729.0 million
Burlington Industries	8.0	640.0 million

Note: Figures represent announcements, not actual purchases, and may include more than one announcement. Values are actual dollar amounts when available or estimates based on closing prices before announcements. Reprinted by permission of *The Wall Street Journal*, Dow Jones and Company, Inc., January 4, 1987, p.8B. All rights reserved. Source: Merrill Lynch & Co.

Stock repurchases: Biggest announced stock buybacks of 1987 / Table 18-7 (final part)

Company	Common Shares (in millions)	Value
Monsanto	8.0	627.0 million
ITT	10.0	625.0 million
Hospital Corp. of America	12.0	612.0 million
Atlantic Richfield	8.3	600.0 million
Schlumberger	20.0	595.0 million
Tektronix	15.6	593.2 million
Boeing	15.0	592.5 million
Kimberly-Clark	9.0	547.5 million
Kraft	10.0	547.5 million
Eaton	8.5	500.0 million
Kmart	17.9	500.0 million

Note: Figures represent announcements, not actual purchases, and may include more than one announcement. Values are actual dollar amounts when available or estimates based on closing prices before announcements. Reprinted by permission of *The Wall Street Journal*, Dow Jones and Company, Inc., January 4, 1987, p.8B. All rights reserved. Source: Merrill Lynch & Co.

BLOCK · HIRT

Foundations
of Financial
Management

EIGHTH EDITION

T-CH19

Chapter 19
Convertibles and Warrants

Convertible Securities
    Value of the Convertible Bond
    Is this Fool's Gold?
    Advantages and Disadvantages to the Corporation
    Forcing Conversion
    Euro-Convertible Bonds

Accounting Considerations with Convertibles

Financing through Warrants
    Valuation of Warrants
    Use of Warrant in Corporate Finance

Accounting Considerations with Warrants

BLOCK · HIRT

Foundations
of Financial
Management

EIGHTH EDITION

T 19-1

Price movement pattern for a convertible bond / Figure 19-1

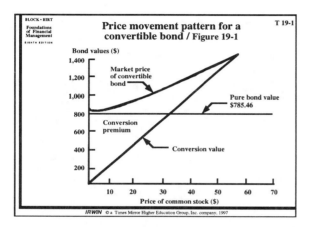

BLOCK · HIRT

Foundations
of Financial
Management

EIGHTH EDITION

T 19-2

Pricing pattern for convertible bonds outstanding, August 1995 / Table 19-1 (first part)

Issue, Coupon, and Maturity	S&P Bond Rating	Conversion Value	Market Value of Bond	Pure Bond Value	Yield to Maturity on Bond	Market Rate for Nonconvertible Bonds of Similar Maturity and Quality
Bank of New York.. 7.5, 2001	A-	$1,969.28	$1,988.80	$1,000	NMF†	7.50%
Bell Sports 4.25, 2000	B	224.30	770.00	770	9.98%	9.98%
CIGNA 8.2, 2010	BBB	1,326.00	1,310.00	1,000	5.19%	8.20%
Convex Computers . 6.0, 2012	NR*	206.90	571.00	570	12.06%	11.44%

*NR = Not rated
†NMF —Yield to maturity assumes that the bond is redeemed at par value. Because these bonds sell at such a high premium compared to par value, the yield to maturity calculates out to be negative. Since these bonds will be converted into common stock and not be redeemed at the lower par value, the yield to maturity is meaningless.
Source: *Value Line Convertibles,* August 14, 1995; *S & P Bond Guide,* September, 1995.

Pricing pattern for convertible bonds outstanding, August 1995 / Table 19-1 (final part)

Issue, Coupon, and Maturity	S&P Bond Rating	Conversion Value	Market Value of Bond	Pure Bond Value	Yield to Maturity on Bond	Market Rate for Nonconvertible Bonds of Similar Maturity and Quality
J.P. Morgan 4.75, 1998	AA+	3,625.00	3,625.00	940	NMF†	6.86%
Norwest Corporation 6.75, 2003	A+	5,575.00	5,492.50	980	NMF†	7.08%
Sterling Software . 5.75, 2003	B+	1,424.10	1,452.60	800	NMF†	9.56%
Time Warner 8.75, 2015	BB+	917.00	1,047.50	1,020	8.25%	8.54%

†NMF —Yield to maturity assumes that the bond is redeemed at par value. Because these bonds sell at such a high premium compared to par value, the yield to maturity calculates out to be negative. Since these bonds will be converted into common stock and not be redeemed at the lower par value, the yield to maturity is meaningless.
Source: *Value Line Convertibles*, August 14, 1995; *S & P Bond Guide*, September, 1995.

Successful convertible bonds not yet called as of September 1995 / Table 19-3

Issue, Coupon, and Maturity	S&P Bond Rating	Current Market Price	Current Call Price	Current Yield	Common Stock Dividend Yield
Bank of New York Co. 7.5, 2001	A-	$1,988.80	$1,037.50	3.37%	3.69%
Deere & Co. 5.5s, 2001	A-	2,678.80	1,002.75	2.10%	2.54%
Hercules Inc. 8.00, 2010	A-	3,733.75	1,000.00	2.14%	1.62%
Lam Research Corp. 6.00, 2003	B	2,410.00	NCB*	2.49%	Nil
Motorola, Inc. Zero coupon, 2009	AA-	1,363.75	411.89†	—	0.52%
Norwest Corp. 6.75, 2003	A+	5,492.50	1,010.13	1.12%	3.44%
Union Pacific 4.75, 1999	A-	9,170.00	1,000.00	0.52%	2.75%

*NCB = non callable bond
†There is a low call price because it is a zero-coupon convertible. The call price will rise as the bond matures.
Source: *Standard & Poor's Bond Guide*, September 1995; *Value Line Convertibles*

Selected issues of convertible Eurobonds, October 1995 / Table 19-4

Issue, Coupon, and Maturity	Moody's Bond Rating	Conversion Value	Market Value of Bond	Call Price
American Brands cv. eurodeb. 7.75, 2002	A2	$1,494.70	$1,503.80	$1,015.50
Genetech, Inc. euro c.s.d. 5.0, 2002	Baa3	567.80	569.60	1,000.00
Termo Instrument Systems cv. eurobond 3.75, 2000	Ba1	1,311.00	1,137.50	NCB*
Texas Instruments euro c.s.d. 2.75, 2002	Baa1	1,701.30	1,701.50	1,017.50

*NCB–non callable bond
Source: *Value Line Convertibles*, October 23, 1995; *Moody's Bond Record*, August 1995

Relationships determining warrant prices, August 1995 / Table 19-6

Firm: Place of Warrant Listing & Stock Listing*	(2) Warrant Price	(3) Stock Price	(4) Exercise Price	(5) Number of Shares	(6) Intrinsic Value	(7) Speculative Premium
Concord Health Group OTC, OTC, due 04/20/00	1.50	5.00	5.50	1.000	None	1.50
Fleet Financial NYSE, NYSE, due 01/26/01	6.25	35.25	43.88	1.000	None	6.25
Glendale Fed. Sav. NYSE, OTC, due 08/21/00	5.50	14.63	12.00	1.000	$2.63	2.87
Intel Corp. (Step Up Warrant)† OTC, OTC, due 03/14/98	35.00	63.50	38.75	1.000	$24.75	10.25
Lone Star Ind. NYSE, NYSE, due 12/31/00	11.63	22.38	18.75	1.000	$3.63	8.00
National Gypsum OTC, due 01/01/00	38.50	53.25	14.50	1.000	$38.75	(0.25)

*OTC = over-the-counter market; NYSE = New York Stock Exchange.
†Exercise price is $38.75 through March 14, 1996; $40.25 through March 15, 1997; and $41.75 through March 14, 1998, the date of expiration.
Source: *Value Line Convertibles*, August 14, 1995.

Market price relationships for a warrant / Figure 19-2

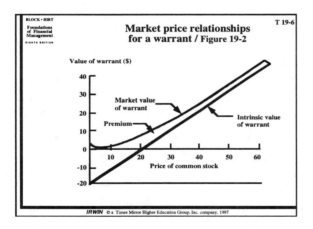

Review of Formulas (first part)

1. Primary earnings per share $= \dfrac{\text{Adjusted earnings after taxes}}{\text{Shares outstanding} + \text{Common stock equivalents}}$ (19-1)

2. Fully diluted earnings per share $= \dfrac{\text{Adjusted earnings after taxes}}{\text{Shares outstanding} + \text{Common stock equivalents} + \textit{All convertibles regardless of the interest rate}}$ (19-2)

BLOCK • HIRT

Foundations
of Financial
Management

EIGHTH EDITION

T 19-7

Review of Formulas (final part)

3. Intrinsic value of a warrant

$$I = (M - E) \times N \qquad (19\text{-}3)$$

where

I = Intrinsic value of a warrant
M = Market value of a common stock
E = Exercise price of a warrant
N = Number of shares each warrant entitles
the holder to purchase

4. Speculative premium of a warrant

$$S = W - I \qquad (19\text{-}4)$$

where

S = Speculative premium
W = Warrant price
I = Intrinsic value

Chapter 20
External Growth Through Mergers

Motives for Business Combinations
   Financial Motives
   Nonfinancial Motives
   Motives of Selling Stockholders

Terms of Exchange
   Cash Purchases
   Stock-for-Stock Exchange
   Portfolio Effect

Accounting Considerations in Mergers and Acquisitions

Negotiated versus Tendered Offers

Premium Offers and Stock Price Movements

Two-Step Buyout

Risk-reduction portfolio
benefits / Figure 20-1

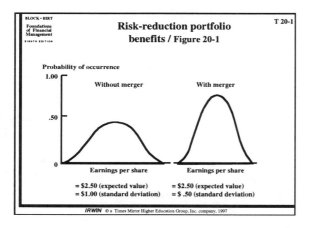

Probability of occurrence

1.00

Without merger   With merger

.50

0

Earnings per share   Earnings per share

= $2.50 (expected value)   = $2.50 (expected value)
= $1.00 (standard deviation)   = $ .50 (standard deviation)

Financial data on potential
merging firms / Table 20-2 (first part)

	Small Corporation	Expand Corporation
Total earnings	$200,000	$500,000
Number of shares of stock outstanding	50,000	200,000
Earnings per share	$4.00	$2.50
Price-earnings ratio (P/E)	7.5x	12x
Market price per share	$30.00	$30.00

BLOCK · HIRT

Foundations
of Financial
Management

EIGHTH EDITION

T 20-2

Postmerger earnings per share / Table 20-3 (final part)

Total earnings: Small ($200,000) + Expand ($500,000)	$700,000
Shares outstanding in surviving corporation: Old (200,000) + New (50,000)	250,000

New earnings per share for Expand Corporation = $\dfrac{\$700,000}{250,000}$ = $2.80

IRWIN © a Times Mirror Higher Education Group, Inc. company, 1997

BLOCK · HIRT

Foundations
of Financial
Management

EIGHTH EDITION

T 20-3

Largest acquisitions of the last decade / Table 20-1

	Acquired Company	Buyer	Cost ($ billions)	Year
1.	RJR Nabisco	Kohlberg Kravis Roberts	$24.7	1989
2.	Capital Cities/ABC	Walt Disney Co.	19.2	1995
3.	McCaw Cellular	AT&T	18.9	1994
4.	Wellcome PLC	Glaxo PLC	15.0	1995
5.	Warner Comm.	Time Inc.	14.1	1990
6.	Kraft	Philip Morris	13.4	1988
7.	Gulf Oil	Chevron	13.3	1984
8.	Squibb	Bristol-Myers	12.1	1989
9.	Getty Oil	Texaco	10.1	1984
10.	Martin Marietta	Lockheed Corp.	10.0	1995
11.	Chase Manhattan	Chemical Banking	10.0	1995
12.	Paramount Com.	Viacom Inc.	9.6	1994

IRWIN © a Times Mirror Higher Education Group, Inc. company, 1997

Chapter 21
International Financial Management

The Multinational Corporation: Nature and Environment

Foreign Exchange Rights

Managing Foreign Exchange Risk

Foreign Investment Decisions

Financing International Business Operations

    Funding of Transactions

    International Equity Markets

    The International Finance Corporation

Some Unsettled Issues in International Finance

Appendix 21-A: Cash Flow Analysis and the Foreign Investment Decision

---

1994 data on international activities of selected U.S. corporations / Table 21-1 (first part)

	Foreign Sales (percent of total sales)	Foreign Operating Profit (percent of total operating profit)	Foreign Assets (percent of total assets)
Chevron	30.1%	61.8%	37.6%
Colgate-Palmolive	68.4	75.6	49.9
CPC International	64.4	54.9	70.6
Digital Equipment	61.7	63.3	52.8
Eastman Kodak	33.8	32.5	52.8
First Chicago Corporation	14.4	10.5	15.7
General Electric	17.0	13.1	18.1
General Motors	21.0	63.3	22.4
Gillette	68.0	68.6	75.7
Goodyear Tire and Rubber	38.9	50.4	40.1
Merck	20.2	27.9	33.5
Mobil	66.2	72.0	63.1
Procter & Gamble	51.5	29.3	59.6
Texaco	50.0	31.1	49.0
Westinghouse	11.0	4.7	5.5

Source: Various 1994 annual reports from the above companies.

Selected currencies and exchange rates / Table 21-2

Dollar (fractions of dollar) that one can exchange for each unit of foreign currency ($/currency)

Country	Currency		Aug. 1, 1990	Jan. 1, 1993	Nov. 16, 1995
Austria	1 schilling	=	$0.0894	$0.0868	$0.1008
Belgium	1 franc	=	0.0260	0.0297	0.0345
Britain	1 pound	=	1.8565	1.5145	1.5558
Denmark	1 krone	=	0.1649	0.1572	0.1829
France	1 franc	=	0.1915	0.1801	0.2056
Germany	1 deutsche mark	=	0.6305	0.6102	0.7092
India	1 rupee	=	0.0571	0.0348	0.0287
Italy	1 lira	=	0.0005	0.0007	0.0006
Japan	1 yen	=	0.0068	0.0081	0.0098
Mexico	1 peso	=	0.3000	0.3206	0.1271
Netherlands	1 guilder	=	0.5587	0.5426	0.6330
Portugal	1 escudo	=	0.0071	0.0068	0.0068
South Africa	1 rand	=	0.3859	0.3263	0.2742
Spain	1 peseta	=	0.0102	0.0086	0.0082
Sweden	1 krona	=	0.1719	0.1388	0.1511
Switzerland	1 franc	=	0.7383	0.6780	0.8757

BLOCK · HIRT
Foundations
of Financial
Management
EIGHTH EDITION

Risk reduction from international diversification / Figure 21-1

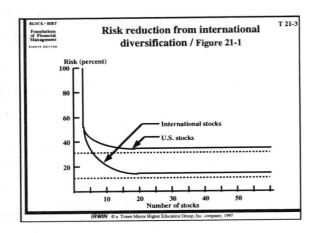

IRWIN © a Times Mirror Higher Education Group, Inc. company, 1997

BLOCK · HIRT
Foundations
of Financial
Management
EIGHTH EDITION

Cash flow analysis of a foreign investment / Table 21A-1 (first part)

Projected Cash Flows (million ringgits unless otherwise stated)

	Year 1	Year 2	Year 3	Year 4	Year 5	Year 6
Revenues	45.00	50.00	55.00	60.00	65.00	70.00
− Operating expenses	28.00	30.00	30.00	32.00	35.00	35.00
− Depreciation	10.00	10.00	10.00	10.00	10.00	10.00
Earnings before Salaysian taxes	7.00	10.00	15.00	18.00	20.00	25.00
−Salaysian income tax (25%)	1.75	2.50	3.75	4.50	5.00	6.25
Earnings after foreign income taxes	5.25	7.50	11.25	13.50	15.00	18.75
= Dividends repatriated	5.25	7.50	11.25	13.50	15.00	18.75

IRWIN © a Times Mirror Higher Education Group, Inc. company, 1997

BLOCK · HIRT
Foundations
of Financial
Management
EIGHTH EDITION

Cash flow analysis of a foreign investment / Table 21A-1 (final part)

Projected Cash Flows (million ringgits unless otherwise stated)

	Year 1	Year 2	Year 3	Year 4	Year 5	Year 6
Gross U.S. taxes (30% of foreign earnings before taxes	2.10	3.00	4.50	5.40	6.00	7.50
− Foreign tax credit	1.75	2.50	3.75	4.50	5.00	6.25
Net U.S. taxes payable	0.35	0.50	0.75	0.90	1.00	1.25
Aftertax dividend received by Tex Systems	4.90	7.00	10.50	12.60	14.00	17.50
Exchange rate (ringgits/$)	2.00	2.04	2.08	2.12	2.16	2.21
Aftertax dividend (U.S. $)	2.45	3.43	5.05	5.94	6.48	7.92
PVıғ (at 20%)	0.833	0.694	0.579	0.482	0.402	0.335
PV of dividends ($)	2.04 +	2.38 +	2.92 +	2.86 +	2.60 +	2.65 = $15.45

IRWIN © a Times Mirror Higher Education Group, Inc. company, 1997